TEAMWORK AND TEAMPLAY

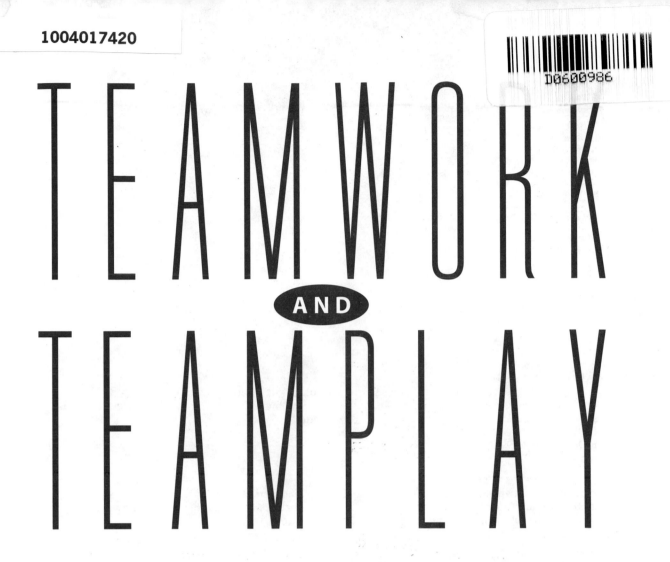

GAMES AND ACTIVITIES FOR BUILDING AND TRAINING TEAMS

Sivasailam "Thiagi" Thiagarajan
Glenn Parker

JOSSEY-BASS/PFEIFFER
A Wiley Company
www.pfeiffer.com

Published by

JOSSEY-BASS/PFEIFFER

A Wiley Company
989 Market Street
San Francisco, CA 94103-1741
415.433.1740; Fax 415.433.0499
800.274.4434; Fax 800.569.0443

www.pfeiffer.com

Jossey-Bass/Pfeiffer is a registered trademark of John Wiley & Sons, Inc.

ISBN: 0-7879-4791-1
Library of Congress Catalog Card Number 99-19287

Library of Congress Cataloging-in-Publication Data

Thiagarajan, Sivasailam.

    Teamwork and teamplay : games and activities for building and
training teams / Sivasailam "Thiagi" Thiagarajan, Glenn Parker.
       p.   cm.
    ISBN 0-7879-4791-1
    1. Teams in the workplace.   2. Teams in the workplace—Training
of. 3. Management games. Problem solving. 4. Group problem
solving. 5. Employee empowerment.   I. Parker, Glenn M., 1938–
II. Title.
HD66.T4665   1999
658.4'02—dc21   99-19287
                                            CIP

Acquiring Editor: *Matthew Holt*
Director of Development: *Kathleen Dolan Davies*
Senior Production Editor: *Pamela Berkman*
Cover Design: *Brenda Duke*

Printed in the United States of America

Printing 10 9 8 7 6 5

We at Jossey-Bass strive to use the most environmentally sensitive paper stocks available to us. Our
publications are printed on acid-free recycled stock whenever possible, and our paper always meets or
exceeds minimum GPO and EPA requirements.

Contents

Introduction

What Is a Team?

Team, unit, crew, club, gang, group, clique, panel, committee, and *task force*—these related words and their alternative definitions frequently confuse people. Our definition of a team is

> a group of people with a high degree of interdependence geared toward the achievement of a goal or the completion of a task.

In other words, members of a team agree on a *goal* and agree that the only way to achieve the goal is to *work together* (Parker, 1990).

Some groups have a common goal but do not work together to achieve it. For example, many management teams are really groups because they can work independently to achieve the goal. Some groups work together but do not have a common goal. For example, most people interact with one another during meetings, but everyone seems to have a different goal. So these meeting participants do not constitute a real team.

Why Learn About Teams?

Teams are becoming increasingly important in today's organizations. Following are some newer types of demands placed on teamwork.

Organizational Structures   During the past decade, traditional hierarchical structures in organizations have been replaced by team-based structures. This change has increased the demand for team-training activities, since it makes more sense to train employees in teams, if they are going to work in teams.

Global Interaction   Technological breakthroughs in communication and travel have reduced physical distance to an insignificant variable and spawned international teams. This development has imposed new demands on teamwork, which involve multicultural participants.

Virtual Interaction   Electronic mail, the Internet, and intranets have created new types of teams whose members have little or no face-to-face interaction. This situation has created a demand for hard skills related to the use of technology and soft skills related to interaction in cyberspace.

Changing Workforce   Employees born in the 1970s and raised on MTV and video games have lifestyles and workstyles different from those of people born earlier.

Teamwork among members of this generation and between different generations has created a demand for new structures and methods.

Increased Empowerment   Around the world, citizens want to get involved in the way politicians make decisions in local and national governments, and employees want to get involved in the way managers make decisions in the workplace. New team techniques are required to involve large masses in real-time strategic change.

Self-Help Groups   People have rediscovered the advantages of receiving and giving training and therapy through the sharing of experiences, insights, and skills with one another. This trend has created a demand for new forms of leaderless teams.

What Are Different Types of Teams?

There are many different types of teams as well as many different words to describe the same type of team. An especially useful catalogue of teams was provided by Peter Scholtes (1996).

1. **Natural Work Groups**   People who work together every day: same office, same location, same machine, and same process.

2. **Business Teams**   Usually a cross-functional team that oversees a specific product line or customer segment.

3. **Management Teams: Executive Teams**   A group of managers who are peers and the person to whom they usually report.

4. **Management Teams: "Linchpin" Teams**   A cascading network of teams starting with the executive team, in which each manager is a member of a team led by his or her boss and leads a team consisting of his or her direct subordinates.

5. **New Product/Service Design Teams**   Usually a cross-functional group assigned to redesign all or part of a product or service.

6. **Process Redesign, or Systems Reengineering, Teams**   Similar to new product/service teams but deals with the internal operations that create and deliver the product or service.

7. **Improvement Project Teams**   A natural work group or cross-functional team whose responsibility is to achieve some needed improvement of an existing process; an ad hoc assignment.

What Are Games and Activities?

Games, activities, simulations, exercises, case studies, experiential learning techniques, role-plays, and *active training sessions*—this is another set of related words with alternative definitions that frequently confuse people. Our definition of an instructional game or an activity is

> a structured process that involves participants interacting with one another to share their experiences and insights.

All games and activities in this book share these two key elements: experience and interaction. Participants take an active role in jointly experiencing an event, reflecting on it, and sharing what they learned from it.

Why Use Games and Activities?

Since teamwork involves participants interacting with one another, it makes sense that they should also learn in situations presented by games and activities. Following are some additional reasons why an interactive experiential approach results in effective learning.

Cognitive Science Research   Studies indicate that people learn more effectively and apply their newly learned knowledge and skills more effectively through games and activities. Research on such diverse areas as stress, anxiety, creativity, and self-efficacy reinforce the generalization that we need to play more in order to improve our learning.

Multiple Intelligences   Recent studies on the nature of intelligence have eliminated traditional IQ measures as the sole indicator of effective performance. Newer frameworks of intelligence emphasize that there are several avenues to learning other than the conventional use of language and logic. Games and activities tap into alternative intelligences.

Adult Learning Theory   Most adults bring a rich store of experiences to the learning situation. The primary task of the facilitator is to help them, through collaborative efforts, to derive generalizations from this base of experience.

Emotional Learning   Events that are accompanied by emotions result in long-lasting learning. Boredom is not conducive to effective learning. Games and activities that include appropriate levels of cooperation within teams and competition across teams add emotional elements to learning.

Practice and Feedback   Learners cannot master skills without repeated practice and feedback. Games and activities provide opportunities for practicing interpersonal skills and for receiving immediate feedback from peers.

What Are Different Types of Activities?

There are several different classification schemes for training activities. In our context of working with teams, it is important to differentiate between team building and team training.

Team building increases the ability of an intact team to work together. The process of team building involves analyzing the strengths and improvement opportunities in a team, building on the current strengths, reducing the ineffective practices, and preparing a plan for ongoing team effectiveness. The team, guided by a facilitator, takes responsibility for the development of the plan and its implementation. A team-building session is attended only by members of a specific team (referred to as an "intact" team) whose members regularly work together to achieve a goal or to accomplish a task. An intact team may be a natural work group or a cross-functional team.

Team training increases the knowledge and skills of the participants in various aspects of teamwork and being a team player. The participants who attend a team-training session may be individuals or groups from a specific team. These participants take back and apply their new skills and knowledge to different teams they belong to.

Some of the activities in this book are best suited for team building while some others are most useful for team training. Some activities may be used for either purpose. An index at the back of this book identifies the best use for each activity.

How to Use the Games and Activities in This Book

All the games and activities in this book have been field-tested by the two of us in our workshops. In addition, several of the activities have also been successfully used by our colleagues and workshop participants. So, you can use the activities with your teams and be assured that they will result in effective learning and performance improvement.

Following are some guidelines to help you get the maximum effect from any of these games and activities:

Before Conducting the Activity

1. Select the most appropriate activity. We have provided several indexes to help you do this. Begin by identifying the activities that match your primary purpose. Decide whether you are working in a team-building or a team-training mode. Then select the specific activity that best matches your available time, number of participants, and other logistic constraints.

2. Review the activity with your client and a few representative participants. If necessary, recruit a co-facilitator to assist you.

3. Conduct a dry run. Walk through the steps of the activity with your co-facilitator. Make suitable adaptations to better suit the needs and preferences of your participants. Review the variations that we have provided for each activity.

4. Estimate the number of participants and collect all the required supplies and materials. Make enough copies of game materials and handouts.

5. Specify the overall goals and objectives for your team-building or team-training session. Decide how to reach additional objectives that are likely to be achieved by the activity.

6. Plan your briefing procedure. Decide whether to present a "lecturette" before conducting the activity. Prepare an outline for this presentation along with suitable visuals.

7. Plan your debriefing procedure. Prepare a list of discussion questions to ensure that participants will reflect on their performance, gain useful insights, and share the learning points with one another. Start with the questions we have included.

8. Anticipate possible disasters. Ask yourself a series of *what-if* questions. Brainstorm preventative steps and contingency plans with your co-facilitator.

9. Anticipate a smooth flow of the activity. Visualize your participants enjoying the activity and learning from it.

During the Activity

1. Get into the activity as quickly as possible. Keep your initial presentations and instructions to a minimum.

2. Present an outline of the important rules and steps of the activity. Assign roles to different participants and distribute the materials.

3. Warn participants that they may be confused initially. Explain that things will become clearer as the activity progresses.

4. Don't interfere with participant behaviors once the activity has begun. Remind participants of the rules when necessary. Implement time limits and other rules in a fair but flexible manner.

5. Move smoothly from one stage of the activity to the next.

6. Bring the activity to a definite conclusion at the end of the assigned time period or when the goal is achieved.

After the Activity

1. Conduct a debriefing discussion. Ask participants to reflect on their performance and share their insights with one another.

2. Ask participants to report on what they learned from the activity. Also ask them for their action plans based on the newly learned procedures and principles.

3. Invite participants to ask you questions about the activity and the learning outcomes. Correct any misconceptions. Add suitable caveats—*conceptual material and/or lessons from your experience*—to prevent participants from going far beyond the data.

4. Suggest suitable follow-up activities.

Always Remember

These games and activities are tools to help you achieve team-building and team-training goals. Keep focused on those goals to prevent an activity from becoming an end in itself.

Be flexible. Although games and activities have rules, don't become obsessed with them. An important requirement for effective teamwork is to maintain your sense of humor and to take serious things playfully.

References

Parker, G. M., *Team players and teamwork*. San Francisco: Jossey-Bass, 1990.

Scholtes, P., *Teams in the Age of Systems*, in G. M. Parker, *Best practices in teams*, vol. 1. Amherst, MA: HRD Press, 1990, pp. 229–251.

About the Authors

Sivasailam "Thiagi" Thiagarajan and Glenn Parker

Thiagi and Glenn are old-school team builders. They believe in designing training and development activities based on data that reflect the needs of the members and the issues faced by the team. They freely share their expertise and experience with colleagues in the field. However, they also feel strongly that, as the architect's maxim goes, "form follows function." That is, it is important to first identify your purpose and then select your methodology. Thiagi and Glenn's work is designed to aid team trainers and developers who have diagnosed needs by providing them with an expanded repertoire of activities and games.

Thiagi and Glenn share a belief in experiential learning and action research. They believe that individuals learn and teams develop by involvement in the change process. Rarely do teams improve by listening to a lecture or reading a book in isolation. Improvement comes from data collection and diagnosis of the current situation followed by problem solving and action planning. Activities in this book and others by Thiagi and Glenn are based on that premise.

Thiagi and Glenn believe that team training and team building can be fun. The development process can be playful, upbeat, and positive. At the same time, the play must be accompanied by thoughtful reflection on the action and its implications for team development. No activity or game should end without time for debriefing.

The authors bring a combined total of more than 60 years of experience to their collaborative efforts. They are both designers of hundreds of exercises, games, and simulations; authors of numerous books; consultants to many organizations; and facilitators of thousands of team-building sessions, training classes, and large group meetings.

This book represents both the culmination of a series of joint projects and the beginning of others. Several years ago Thiagi and Glenn collaborated on a major simulation game, *Cross-Functional Teams: The Simulation Game*. Later, they teamed up on a board game based on the *Parker Team Player Survey* called *Team Players: A Game for Exploring Team Player Styles*. They also jointly lead a one-day workshop, *Games and Activities for Building and Training Teams*.

For information on their work, including lots of free activities, articles, and information, access their web sites: **www.thiagi.com** and **www.glennparker.com**.

Glenn Parker

Author and consultant Glenn Parker works with organizations to create and sustain high-performing teams, effective team players, and team-based systems. His best-selling book, *Team Players and Teamwork* (Jossey-Bass, 1990), was selected as one of the ten best business books of 1990. Now in its seventh printing, *Team Players and Teamwork* has been published in several other languages and has been brought to the screen in an exciting new video, *Team Building: What Makes a Good Team Player?* (CRM Films, 1995). His training and team-building instruments, the *Parker Team Player Survey* (Xicom, 1991) and the *Team Development Survey* (Xicom, 1992), have become the standards in the field.

Glenn is co-author of *50 Activities for Team Building*, v. 1 (HRD Press, 1991), which was selected by Human Resource Executives as one of 1992's Top Ten Training Tools. He is the author of three resources for cross-functional teams: (1) the book, *Cross-Functional Teams: Working with Allies, Enemies and Other Strangers* (Jossey-Bass, 1994), which has been called "a must for anyone charged with managing the future of the business" and is a selection of the Executive Program Book Club and Soundview Executive Book Summaries; (2) the new manual, *Cross-Functional Teams Toolkit* (Pfeiffer, 1997); and (3) *Cross-Functional Teams: The Simulation Game*, which he co-developed (Xicom, 1998). Glenn is co-author of *50 Activities for Self-Directed Teams* (HRD Press, 1994) and author of a collection of training resources and job aids, *The Team Kit* (HRD Press, 1995). He is also editor of the HRD *Press Best Practices for Teams*, vol. 1 (1996) and vol. 2 (1998). His latest publication is *25 Instruments for Team Building* (HRD Press, 1998).

Glenn does not just write about teamwork. He is a hands-on consultant and trainer who works with start-up and ongoing teams of all types in a variety of industries. He facilitates team building, conducts training workshops, consults with management, and gives presentations for organizations across a wide variety of industries. His clients have included pharmaceutical companies such as Merck and Company, Johnson & Johnson, Bristol-Myers Squibb, Hoffmann-La Roche, Rhône-Poulenc Rorer, Novo Nordisk, and Ciba-Geigy; a variety of industrial organizations such as 3M, Kimberly-Clark, The Budd Company, Penntech Papers, Allied Signal, Pratt & Whitney, LEGO, BOC Gases, and Sun MicroSystems; companies in telecommunications including AT&T, Pacific Bell, NYNEX, Lucent, Bellcore, and Siemens/ROLM Communications; service businesses such as Commerce Clearing House's Legal Information Service, Asea Brown Boveri (ABB) Environmental Services, American Express, Promus Hotel Corporation (Embassy Suites, Hampton Inns), and the *New England Journal of Medicine*; the sales and marketing organizations of Roche Laboratories and Pontiac Division of General Motors; health care providers such as Aurora Health Center, Pocono Medical Center, St. Rita's Medical Center, Monmouth Medical Center, and Riverside Health Care Center; retailers such as Ann Taylor, and several government agencies such as Department of Navy, Environmental Protection Agency, and National Institutes of Health.

Glenn holds a B.A. from City College of New York, an M.A. from the University of Illinois, and has studied for the doctorate at Cornell University. He is much in demand as a speaker at corporate meetings and at national conferences sponsored by the American Society for Training and Development (ASTD), Lakewood Conferences, and Center for the Study of Work Teams. He was a keynote speaker at the BEST OF TEAMS '98 Conference. He is past president of the ASTD Mid-New Jersey chapter and currently chairs the ASTD Publishing Review Committee.

Glenn is the father of three grown children and currently lives in Lawrenceville, New Jersey, with his wife Judy. In his spare time he rides his bike, volunteers with the American Cancer Society, roots for the Philadelphia 76ers, and plans his next vacation.

Sivasailam Thiagarajan

Dr. Sivasailam "Thiagi" Thiagarajan works with corporate managers and employees to improve the organization's performance, productivity, and profits.

Thiagi's long-term clients include AT&T, Arthur Anderson, Chevron, Harris Bank, IBM, Intel, Intelsat, and Liberty Mutual. On a short-term basis, he has worked with more than 50 different organizations in high-tech, financial services, and management consulting. For these clients, Thiagi has consulted and conducted training in such areas as rightsizing, diversity, teamwork, customer satisfaction, total quality management, and organizational learning.

Thiagi has published 20 books and more than 200 articles. He a member of the editorial boards of *Simulation and Gaming* and *Educational Technology*. Recently, he has published *Games By Thiagi* (HRD Press, 1995), a set of 17 books containing some 50 games and activities in such areas as diversity, leadership, customer satisfaction, trust, and teamwork. He also writes a monthly newsletter, the *Thiagi GameLetter*, published by Jossey-Bass/Pfeiffer.

Thiagi has conducted workshops, made presentations, and given keynote addresses at hundreds of corporate meetings and professional conferences including Lakewood Conferences, American Society for Training and Development (ASTD), and International Society for Performance Improvement (ISPI). His sessions are always lively, interactive, challenging, and fun.

Thiagi is a past president of the North American Simulation and Gaming Association (NASAGA), National Society for Performance and Instruction (NSPI), and the Association for Special Education Technology (ASET). He has received several awards in recognition of his professional contributions including *Honorary Life Member* from NSPI and NASAGA.

Thiagi holds a Ph.D. from Indiana University in instructional systems technology and has taught at the university in the same field. Internationally recognized as an expert in multinational collaboration and active learning in organizations, Thiagi has lived and worked in three different countries and has consulted in 21 others. Thiagi lives in Bloomington, Indiana, with his wife Lucy, who teaches in a Montessori school, and his son Raja, who designs computer games and web pages. In his spare time, Thiagi reads murder mysteries, writes short stories, performs magic tricks, and works with community action groups in Madras, India.

This is a fun way to break up a serious and intense team-building meeting and yet stay on track.

BALLOONATICS
A Not-So-Serious Assessment Activity

Purpose:

1. To provide a team or participants in a training class with a lighthearted activity
2. To provide a non-intensive opportunity to give feedback on the organization's culture
3. To have fun

Team Size:

Works well with an intact team of less than 10, a typical class of 15 to 20 participants, or a large conference group of up to 100

Required Resources:

1. Sufficient copies of each of the Balloonatics
2. A transparency copy of each of the Balloonatics
3. A projector pen for each team
4. Overhead projector and screen

Time:

30 to 45 minutes

Room Setup:

Rectangular table at the front of the room with the projector placed on it; clusters of chairs and tables for each team around the room

Steps:

1. Explain the purpose of the session emphasizing both the serious and fun aspects of the activity.

2. Distribute a transparency copy of one Balloonatic to each team along with a projector pen. Each team will get a different Balloonatic. Provide each team member with a paper copy of the same Balloonatic.

3. Explain that you want each team to come up with words, phrases, sentences, questions, or comments for each of the blanks. The responses should be reflective of the team or organization's culture at this moment in time. Humor is encouraged. Allow 10 to 15 minutes. The consensus wording should be printed on the transparency copy. Each team should select a spokesperson to present its Balloonatic.

4. Each team, in turn, presents its Balloonatic, supported by any necessary explanations, on the overhead projector.

Debriefing:

Conclude by asking the group to provide comments that focus on what this activity tells us about our team or organization. Depending on the nature of the group and the time available, you may debrief after each presentation or only after all Balloonatics have been presented. Here are some possible questions:

- What does this say about our culture in terms of
  —the way we make decisions?
  —how we treat one another?
  —leadership?
  —support of teamwork?
  —rewards and recognition?
  —the way we resolve conflict?
  —availability of resources?
  —the way we solve problems?
  —how we treat customers?
- What aspects of our culture need to change? In what way should things change?
- How would you change your Balloonatic to reflect your desired culture?
- What are some other ways these Balloonatics might be used?

Variations:

1. If time permits, give each team five Balloonatics, and ask them to provide words for all five. Compare the teams responses.

2. Working with a small intact team, you can give each person a different Balloonatic.

We gratefully acknowledge the artists at *Today's TEAM®*, Wentworth Publishing, Lancaster, PA for creating the Balloonatics. Used with permission.

This is a quick icebreaker that demonstrates the value of teamwork.

BOXED IN
AN OPENING ACTIVITY

Purpose:
1. To demonstrate the value of pooling ideas in a team setting
2. To get participants involved in a challenging problem-solving exercise
3. To show the importance of looking at a problem from different perspectives

Team Size:
A team of 4 to 6 members or a large group divided into sub-groups of 4 to 6 each

Required Resources:
1. A transparency of "How Many Boxes Do You See?" (p. 11)
2. An overhead projector and screen

Time:
30 minutes

Room Setup:
Chairs around a U-shaped set of tables, or small clusters of chairs and tables around the room

Steps:
1. With little introduction, display the transparency on the screen.
2. Ask each person to answer the question, "How many square boxes do you see up there?" Be clear that this is an individual activity; that it is to be done privately. When the participant has an answer, he or she should write it on a piece of paper making sure that no one can see the number.

3. When everyone indicates that he or she has written down an answer, organize the participants into teams of 4 to 6 each. Ask everyone to work as a team to reach a consensus on the correct answer. Allow about 10 minutes.

4. First ask what number each person wrote down as his or her answer. Keep a tally on how many different answers were in the group. Then ask, "There were (*for example*) eight different answers to the question. Why were there so many different answers?" Some typical responses:

   - We look at things in a different way.
   - We have different backgrounds.
   - Our training differs.
   - We may have had different interpretations of the problem.
   - The instructions were not clear (the transparency says "how many boxes," but you said "square boxes").

Follow up with this probe: "Do you think it helps or hinders teamwork that there were many different answers for many different reasons?" Clearly, the answer is positive.

5. Ask for the team consensus answer. Ask the team with the correct answer or most correct to come to the projector and show how they got that number. (By the way, the correct answer is 55.)

Debriefing:

Conclude by asking the group to brainstorm key aspects of teamwork that they will take away from this activity. Possible questions to stimulate brainstorming include:

- What did this activity demonstrate about teamwork?
- What lessons will you take away from this activity that you could apply to your own team?
- What can individual team members do to stimulate or support effective teamwork?

Probe for more specifics about the items after the brainstorming phase. Post the responses on the flip chart as "Teamwork Takeaways."

Variations:

1. If time permits, ask the teams to meet again for a few minutes to identify the behaviors that helped them solve the problem.

2. To speed up the activity, omit the individual step and go right to the team problem-solving step.

HOW MANY BOXES DO YOU SEE?

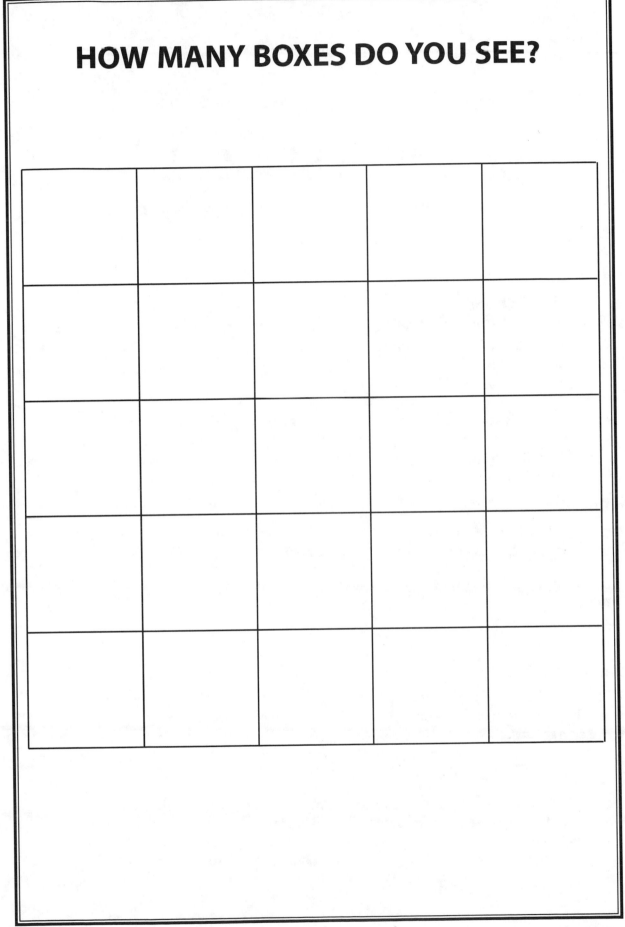

A practical, step-by-step process for gaining support from critical external players.

BUILDING BRIDGES
CREATING EFFECTIVE STAKEHOLDER RELATIONSHIPS

Purpose:

1. To identify the team's key stakeholders
2. To identify the barriers to effective relationships with the key stakeholders
3. To create a plan to develop a positive relationship with the team's stakeholders

Team Size:

Designed primarily for an intact team of 10 or less. However, this activity can be a useful exercise in a team-training workshop for team leaders. Each person completes the form individually and then shares the results with one or two of the other participants.

Required Resources:

1. A copy of the "Building Bridges" handout for each person (p. 14)
2. Flip chart, pad, markers, masking tape or push pins

Time:

2 to 2 1/2 hours

Room Setup:

Moveable chairs set around a table in a room with sufficient space to allow at least three sub-groups to work privately. Alternatively, small break-out rooms can be used for the sub-groups.

Steps:

1. Explain the purpose of the session and the importance of positive relationships with stakeholders to the success of the team. A stakeholder is a person (or a group of people) that has a "stake" in the team's goals and can provide (or can withhold) support, resources, access, and other things the team needs to be successful.

2. Use brainstorming to develop a list of the team's stakeholders. Use consensus or a simple voting method to reduce the list to the team's three most important stakeholders.

3. Distribute the handout "Building Bridges" to each person. Briefly review the items.

4. Form three sub-groups to address the three key stakeholders identified in step 2. Suggest that people opt for the stakeholder of their choice, making sure that there is fairly even distribution among the three groups.

5. Explain that each group's assignment is to complete the form for its designated stakeholder. Give each team a few sheets of flip-chart paper, some markers, and tape or push pins. Indicate that the reports should be prepared on the flip-chart paper. Allow 30 to 45 minutes for this activity.

6. Reassemble the team. Ask each sub-group to present its report. Facilitate a discussion to ensure clarification and reach agreement on the approach.

Debriefing:

Close the session by achieving agreement on the next steps and a date for follow-up to check on progress in implementing the plans. Possible questions include:

- What are the specific things we need to do after this meeting?
- Who shall take responsibility for these things?
- When should we get together again to review progress?
- How do you feel about this exercise?
    —Is it realistic?
    —practical?
    —potentially successsful?

Variations:

1. Instead of the flip-chart paper, make three transparencies of the handout and give one to each sub-group along with a projector pen. Ask each group to prepare its report on the transparency and present it on the overhead projector.

2. As a follow-up exercise, ask the sub-groups to discuss their plans with the stakeholder.

3. If there is insufficient time, simply form the sub-groups and ask them to prepare their plans outside of class and present them at the next team meeting.

BUILDING BRIDGES

1. Identify *a person, department, team or other stakeholder* that your team needs to develop a successful relationship with in order to be successful.

2. What *specific types of help* do you need from this stakeholder?

3. What kinds of *assistance* or input does this stakeholder need from your team?

4. Identify *common objectives* you share with this stakeholder.

5. What *potential barriers* may prevent this stakeholder and your team from working together effectively?

6. What member of your team would be the *best person to be the main contact* with this stakeholder?

7. What *specific steps* can you take to develop a positive relationship and obtain the necessary assistance from this stakeholder?

Can you cooperate to compete?

CENSORSHIP
EXPLORING COOPERATION AND COMPETITION

Purpose:
1. To reinforce basic teamwork concepts
2. To explore situations in which cooperation with others gives us a competitive edge

Team Size:
Works best with 4 to 7 members in each team

Required Resources:
1. Game cards with teamwork concepts. Each card has a key word or phrase. It also has a list of prohibited words or phrases. You may use the set of 12 cards on page 17 or create your own cards.
2. Poker chips (in a bowl)
3. Timer

Time:
15 minutes to 1 hour; you can specify the exact time. The player with the most poker chips at the end of this time wins the game.

Room Setup:
Chairs around a table with the bowl of poker chips in the middle

Steps:
1. Select a player to be the first "definer." Ask the definer to pick a game card and read it silently.
2. The player seated to the left of the definer is the "censor." Ask the definer to show the card to the censor, holding it in such a way that only the definer and the censor can see it.
3. Ask a player to set the timer for 1 minute and start it.

4. Ask the definer to describe the key word or phrase to the other players without using:
   - the key word or phrase.
   - any of the prohibited words or phrases.
   - any part of one of these words or phrases.
   - other forms of these words.

   For example, if *culture* is the prohibited word, the definer should not use any of these words: *cultural, cultured, enculturation, uncultured, culturing,* and *cultures.*

5. While the definer is talking, ask the other players to guess the key word or phrase and shout out their guesses.

6. If the definer uses any form of the key word or prohibited words, the censor yells, "Foul!" The round ends immediately. Nobody scores any points.

7. If a player shouts out the correct term, the censor says "Done!" and shows the card.

8. The definer and the player who correctly guessed the key word each pick a poker chip as their reward.

9. If the definer runs out of time, nobody gets a reward. The censor shows the card to everyone and puts it in a waste pile.

10. Select another player to be the definer. Repeat the same procedure until the players run out of time or game cards. The player with the most poker chips wins the game.

Debriefing:

To maximize the learning outcomes from this game, conduct a debriefing discussion. Here are some suggested questions:

- Is this a game of cooperation (between the definer and the guesser) or of competition (among the definers)?

- This game involves forming temporary partnerships. What similar temporary partnerships do you form in your team?

- Some people withhold shouting out the answer even after they have correctly guessed it. What do you think motivates this behavior? Does something like this ever happen in your team?

- How would your behavior change if we were keeping track of the total poker chips won at each table and identifying the winning team with the most chips? How can you apply this shift from individual victories to team victories in your workplace?

Variations:

Ask the definer to draw a series of pictures to convey the key term in the game card. Eliminate the censor role. The definer and correct guesser each win a poker chip.

Key phrase: *virtual team* **Prohibited:** face to face, e-mail, direct, dispersed, meet	**Key phrase:** *celebration* **Prohibited:** reward, party, ceremony, holiday, success
Key phrase: *facilitator* **Prohibited:** leader, help, consultant, outsider, process	**Key phrase:** *coaching* **Prohibited:** expert, mentor, guidance, advisor, sports
Key phrase: *cross-functional team* **Prohibited:** different, organization, departments, competencies, interests	**Key phrase:** *brainstorming* **Prohibited:** generating ideas, group, fast, evaluation
Key phrase: *consensus* **Prohibited:** agreement, common decision, consent, polling, voting	**Key phrase:** *meetings* **Prohibited:** agenda, waste, decision making, sharing, minutes
Key phrase: *conflict* **Prohibited:** dispute, disagreement, resolutions, confrontation, difference	**Key phrase:** *mission* **Prohibited:** goal, vision, statement, purpose, why
Key phrase: *feedback* **Prohibited:** reaction, information, consequence, loop, constructive	**Key phrase:** *decision making* **Prohibited:** settlement, choice, voting, selection, alternatives

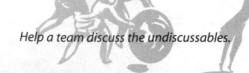

Help a team discuss the undiscussables.

CONTROVERSY
DISCUSSING SENSITIVE TOPICS

Purpose:

1. To conduct an open discussion of controversial topics among team members
2. To understand opposing points of view on a controversial topic

Team Size:

6 or more

Required Resources:

1. A copy of the 9-point *Attitude Scale* for each participant (p. 21)
2. Flip chart
3. Markers

Time:

45 minutes

Room Setup:

Chairs around tables for the first part; open space for the second part

Steps:

1. **Brief the team members.** Introduce the controversial issue briefly, and explain how it is affecting teamwork. Point out the need for an open discussion, and explain that you are going to use a structured approach that will protect team members' privacy.

2. **Specify a proposition.** With inputs from team members, write a proposition on a flip chart. Use a simple, short statement. Keep it easy to understand by avoiding complicated qualifications, politically incorrect phraseology, and negative constructions. For example, use "Team members do their fair share of work" instead of "Some team members appear not to contribute their fair (as perceived by a majority of the other team members) share of overall effort during some of the team's activities."

3. **Establish a baseline.** Distribute copies of the attitude scale to each team member. Ask each participant to check a number on the scale to indicate his or her personal reaction to the proposition on the flip chart. Ask participants not to write their names, and reassure them that they will not be asked to reveal their attitudes to anyone else during this activity.

4. **Compute the statistics.** Collect the attitude scales and ask one or two participants to compute the average value.

5. **Ask for predictions.** Ask everyone to think about the issue and about the probable reactions of the team members toward the issue. Each team member should write a prediction of the average attitude score on the 9-point scale, correct to two decimal places. For example, team members should write 5.00 or 5.01 rather than 5.

6. **Announce the results.** Ask the participants who calculated the average to announce its value. Identify the person who made the closest prediction, and congratulate him or her for psychic ability. Also announce the range of scores (the lowest and the highest numbers checked on the attitude scale).

7. **Form three groups.** Divide the team members into three random groups. Ask the members of one group to assume that their attitude score is 1 (extremely negative), members of another group to assume that their attitude score is 9 (extremely positive), and members of the last group to assume that their attitude score is 5 (neutral).

8. **Prepare for a debate.** Ask the negative and the positive groups to spend the next 5 minutes making a list of arguments in support of their positions. During the same time period, ask the neutral group to prepare a two-column list of both positive and negative arguments. Ask all participants to put aside their personal attitudes and seriously take on the role assigned to them while preparing the lists of arguments.

9. **Conduct the debate.** After 5 minutes, ask members of the positive group to stand on one side of the room and members of the negative group to stand on the opposite side. Ask the members of the neutral team to be seated in the middle of the room. Explain the debate format:

   - The opposing teams will take turns making statements related to the issue, referring to their prepared list of arguments.
   - The statements should be short 5-second sound bites rather than elaborate explanations.
   - They need not be logical rebuttals of the previous statement made by the opposing team.
   - Group members do not have to stick to their list of arguments; they can make spontaneous comments whenever they want.

   Randomly select one group and ask it to start the debate. Stop the debate when you hear too many repetitions or pauses.

10. **Ask the neutral group for their inputs.** Ask members of the neutral group to read their list of arguments on both sides. Then ask them to evaluate the two opposing teams' performance and decide which team did a more credible job. Congratulate the winning team.

Debriefing:

1. Ask participants to reflect on the information, opinions, and perceptions presented during the debate. Invite participants to jot down any notes for their personal reference. Pause for a suitable period of time.

2. Conduct a question-and-answer session. Invite participants to ask questions related to different aspects of the topic. Respond briefly, objectively, and factually to these questions.

3. Facilitate a discussion on how the team should address the topic in everyday terms. Develop norms to deal with members who do not do their fair share.

Variations:

1. Skip the attitude-testing phase and move directly to forming the three groups and preparing for the debate.

2. Instead of conducting a debate, ask each group to write its arguments on one or more flip-chart sheets and tape them to the wall. Invite all team members to review these posters.

3. Follow up this activity with a presentation from a knowledgeable outsider.

ATTITUDE SCALE

_____ 1 Very strongly disagree

_____ 2 Strongly disagree

_____ 3 Disagree

_____ 4 Slightly disagree

_____ 5 Neutral

_____ 6 Slightly agree

_____ 7 Agree

_____ 8 Strongly agree

_____ 9 Very strongly agree

Here's a tough but realistic dilemma for a team.

DEFINING MOMENT
An Ethical Decision-Making Activity

Purpose:
1. To increase a team's awareness of its ethical values
2. To help a team work through the process of making an ethical decision

Team Size:
Ideal for an intact team of 10 members or less. It is also applicable to a team-training group of unrelated participants. If the group is large, this activity can be done in several small sub-groups.

Required Resources:
A copy of the "Defining Moment Case Study" for each person (p. 24)

Time:
1 hour

Room Setup:
Chairs in a circle or around a table. If the group is large, use clusters of tables set around the room.

Steps:
1. Review the purpose of the session.
2. Distribute the handout "Defining Moment." Provide some time for each person to read the case. Respond to all requests for clarification.
3. Facilitate a discussion using some or all of the following questions:
   - What is the ethical dilemma faced by the team?
   - Who are the key stakeholders who may be affected by the decisions, and what are their possible concerns?
   - Are there any possible legal issues involved in the case?

- Does the dilemma violate any company policies, cultural norms, or code of ethics?
- Does the issue impinge on any of your personal values?
- Could you, without hesitation, disclose your decision to your boss, your family, or a newspaper reporter?

If you are using several sub-groups, post these questions on a flip chart or transparency, or prepare a handout.

4. Ask the team to come to a decision about the case.

Debriefing:

After the team has made a decision, facilitate a discussion using the following questions:

- What is your decision?
- What is your justification for the decision?
- What did you learn about ethical decision making from this activity?
- How can you apply this new knowledge to future dilemmas?

Variations:

1. Edit the case to ensure it is relevant to your team.
2. Turn the exercise into a debate. Form two sub-groups, giving one group the task of arguing for telling the customer of their concerns and the other group the task of keeping the information confidential.

DEFINING MOMENT
CASE STUDY

Directions: Please read the case carefully, and decide what the team should do and why.

The product that your team developed and now maintains has been replaced by a new version. Despite efforts to assure that the new product will have all the capabilities of the old version plus some new enhancements, it does not.

The team is very much aware of this as a result of several pilot tests of the new product. Via the team leader, the team has complained to management and made a strong appeal to either go back to the old product or pull the new product back for rework and further development. However, management has refused, saying the problems are being worked and will be fixed in due time. In addition, it is clear that the company has built into its financial projections the added revenue to be generated by this new product. Management also says that in tests at customer sites, no complaints have been raised by customers.

The team knows that if a customer did complain, management would "pull" the product immediately. The team is meeting today to prepare for an on-site visit to one of their largest customers. They are anticipating a question from one of the customer representatives at the meeting, asking how the team likes the new product because they value the team's expertise.

If the team is asked by a customer in the meeting how it likes the product, how should the team respond?

Tired of all those serious survival games? Here's a spoof that teaches the same consensus principles.

ESCAPE FROM GILLIGAN'S ISLAND

A CONSENSUS-BUILDING EXERCISE

Purpose:

1. To demonstrate the value of collaboration among team members
2. To teach the process of consensus decision making

Team Size:

Designed for an intact team of less than 10 people. However, it can be effective with a larger group that has been divided into a series of small sub-teams. In this setting, the sub-teams can compete against one another for the best team score.

Required Resources:

1. A copy of the "Escape from Gilligan's Island: Ranking Sheet" for each person (p. 28)
2. A copy of the "Escape from Gilligan's Island: The Expert's Ranking" for each person (p. 29)
3. A copy of the "Escape from Gilligan's Island: Process Review" for each person (p. 30)
4. A copy of "Do We Have a Consensus?" for each person (p. 31)
5. Flip chart, pad, markers, tape or push pins

Room Setup:

Chairs set around a rectangular or round table. If there are several sub-teams in the session, break-out rooms should be used, or chairs and tables for each sub-team should be set up around a large room so that the discussions can be private.

Time:

1 1/2 to 2 hours divided approximately as follows:

—Introduction and individual ranking: 20 minutes

—Team ranking: 30 minutes

—Scoring: 1–20 minutes

—Process discussion: 30–45 minutes

—Summary: 10–15 minutes

Steps:

1. Explain the purpose and format of the session. If the group is not already set up in teams, form sub-teams of less than 10 each.

2. Distribute the "Escape from Gilligan's Island: Ranking Sheet" to each person. Ask each person to individually rank the 10 items and write the ranking in the first column.

3. Instruct the teams to come to an agreement on their team ranking of the items and write the ranking in the second column. Make it clear that they have 30 minutes to complete the ranking.

4. Distribute the "Escape from Gilligan's Island: The Expert's Ranking." Ask people to fill in the third column on the first form with the expert's ranking and then compute columns 4 and 5. Ask one person from the team to also compute the average individual score. If there are several teams in the session, you should post the scores on the flip chart as follows:

	Team A	Team B	Team C	Team D
1. Average Individual Score				
2. Team Score (Column 5)				
3. Difference Between 1 & 2				

5. Facilitate a discussion on the reasons for the difference between the average individual score and the team score.

   • Did the team do better than the individuals? If so, why? If not, why not?

   • Did one person have a better score than the team? Why did this happen?

Debriefing:

Distribute the "Escape from Gilligan's Island: Process Review." Ask each person to complete the form. Then facilitate a discussion of the answers. Post the responses to the last question on the flip chart. If there are sub-teams in the session, ask one person at each table to serve as facilitator.

- Close the session by asking people to share their key learnings about reaching a consensus. Post the responses on the flip chart; then distribute the "Do We Have a Consensus?" handout and discuss the items.

Variations:

1. It is often better to do the process review before the scoring. In this way, the participants are not influenced by the results but simply discuss the effectiveness of the process.

2. You can distribute the "Do We Have a Consensus?" handout before the team ranking exercise. In this way, the team can practice using the technique during the session.

ESCAPE FROM GILLIGAN'S ISLAND: RANKING SHEET

	COLUMN 1 Individual Ranking	COLUMN 2 Team Ranking	COLUMN 3 Expert's Ranking	COLUMN 4 Difference Between Columns 1 & 3	COLUMN 5 Difference Between Columns 2 & 3
Repair the S.S. Minnow and set sail again					
Use the raft constructed by the skipper to send Mary Ann for help					
Rebuild the control tower and signal ships going by					
Spread some of the Professor's fluorescent dye on the water					
Use Thurston Howell's golf clubs to wave to ships and planes that go by					
Use the Black Morning Spider as a raft and send Gilligan to find help					
Shine the gold from the gold mine and use it as reflector to signal ships and planes					
Ask the Skipper to order a pizza for delivery and ask the delivery person to send help					
Get the Professor to create a musical instrument from coconuts to signal passing ships					
Ask Ginger to use fabric from one of her outfits to create a signal flag					
			TOTALS		

ESCAPE FROM GILLIGAN'S ISLAND: THE EXPERT'S RANKING

1   **Shine the gold...**Survival experts agree that your best strategy is to stay put and try to signal others to rescue you.

2   **Spread some of the professor's dye...**It's another way of signaling possible rescuers.

3   **Ask Ginger to use fabric...**Although it will be tough to get her to part with the fabric (you never know when the dress might be needed for a party), a big flag can be a good signaling device.

4   **Use Thurston Howell's golf clubs...**Although small, the clubs are made of metal and can reflect sunlight, but, then again, Thurston could possibly miss out on a good foursome at the country club.

5   **Rebuild the control tower...**The tower has the advantage of height but needs to be combined with a signaling device. Perhaps Gilligan could stand up there waving his arms.

6   **Get the professor to create a musical instrument...**Another signaling device but useful only if a ship is nearby or Ginger can play "Anchors Away."

7   **Repair the S.S. Minnow...**A good idea but not likely to happen, and what if they get it going only to have it break down again far away from land? They could end up on Fantasy Island.

8   **Use the raft constructed by the skipper...**They should not send anyone by him- or herself—and certainly not Mary Ann.

9   **Use the Black Morning Spider...**The spider is too old, and Gilligan is too dumb to make this work.

10   **Ask the Skipper to order...**Domino's delivers now but not then.

ESCAPE FROM GILLIGAN'S ISLAND: PROCESS REVIEW

1. What did the team do that facilitated the reaching of a consensus?

2. What did the team do that hindered the reaching of a consensus?

3. What did you personally do that either helped or hindered the process?

4. What are some Do's and Don't's guidelines for reaching a consensus that should be adopted by our team?

DO WE HAVE A CONSENSUS?

Directions: After your team has spent some time discussing the pros and cons of a particular issue, ask each team member how he or she feels about the proposed decision that's on the table by selecting one of these 5 options:

❏ I can say an unqualified "yes" to the decision.

❏ I find the decision acceptable.

❏ I can live with the decision, but I'm not especially enthusiastic about it.

❏ I do not fully agree with the decision, but I do not choose to block it.

❏ I do not agree with the decision, and I feel we should explore other options.

If all the responses from team members are 1, 2, 3, or 4, you have a consensus and are ready to move on.

This handout originally appeared in Glenn Parker, *Teamwork: Action steps for building powerful teams*. Aurora, IL: Successories, 1998.

Begin with individual brainstorming and end with a team product.

ET

EXPLORING CHARACTERISTICS OF EFFECTIVE TEAMS

Purpose:

1. To identify characteristics of effective teams
2. To work cooperatively and creatively in self-selected teams

Team Size:

10 to 50 participants form themselves into teams of 3 to 7 members

Required Resources:

1. 20 or more index cards with different characteristics of effective teams. Copy items from the list on page 35.
2. 4 blank index cards for each participant

Time:

45 minutes

Room Setup:

Chairs arranged around rectangular or round tables

Steps:

1. **Get started.** Begin the game quickly. Tell the participants, "I'd like to begin right off with a team activity that will help us get to know one another. It will also allow us to explore the characteristics of effective teams."
2. **Write cards.** Hand out four blank index cards to each participant. Ask them to write down one characteristic of effective teams on each card. The characteristics could be based on the participants' personal experiences or on what they have read.
3. **Distribute cards.** After about 3 minutes, collect opinion cards from participants. Add your prepared cards to this pile. Mix the cards well and give three cards to

each participant. Ask the participants to study the team characteristics and arrange them according to their personal evaluation—from the most to the least powerful characteristic.

4. **Exchange cards.** Arrange the remaining opinion cards on a large table at one side of the room. Tell the participants that they may discard cards from their hands and pick up better replacements. Participants must work silently; they should not talk to one another during this phase of the game. At the end of this exchange, each participant should have three cards that may or may not include cards from the original set.

5. **Swap cards.** Instruct participants to exchange cards with one another to make their hands better reflect their personal opinions about the characteristics of effective teams. In this phase, any participant may swap cards with any other participant; every participant must exchange at least one card.

6. **Form teams.** Ask participants to compare their cards with others' and to form teams with people holding similar cards. Each team should have at least three and not more than seven members. The team must reduce its total number of cards to three. It must discard all other cards, and the three cards it keeps must meet with everyone's approval.

7. **Prepare posters.** Ask each team to prepare a graphic poster that reflects its three final cards. This poster should not include any text.

8. **Present the posters.** After 5 minutes, select a team at random and ask it to come to the front of the room. This team silently displays its poster, and members of the other teams guess aloud the characteristics of effective teams depicted in the poster. After 15 seconds, members of the display team read the characteristics listed in their three selected cards. Other teams take turns to make their presentations, using the same procedure.

Debriefing:

To maximize the learning outcomes from this activity, conduct a brief discussion session. Here are some suggested questions:

- What common themes emerge from the different posters?
- Use the three characteristics as a benchmark for your own team's effectiveness. How does your team rate on each of these characteristics?
- Which team characteristic is the most powerful one for improving its effectiveness?
- Which characteristic do the teams have the least control of?
- Will the team-effectiveness characteristics change from one situation to another? If so, in what way?

Variations:

1. Use a set of prepared team-characteristics cards instead of asking the participants to write their own cards.

2. Ask participants to write a jingle incorporating their three final selections and to sing it instead of preparing and presenting a poster.

3. Ask participants to prepare and present a scenario that incorporates their three final selections.

CHARACTERISTICS OF EFFECTIVE TEAMS

1. A clear goal

2. A focus on achieving results

3. A plan for reaching the goal

4. Clear roles

5. Commitment to the goal

6. Competent members

7. Decision by consensus

8. Diversity among team members

9. Effective interpersonal skills

10. Effective stakeholder relationships

11. Empowerment

12. High standards of excellence

13. Informal climate

14. Management support

15. Openness to new ideas

16. Periodic self-assessment

17. Recognition for team member accomplishments

18. Shared leadership

19. Small size

20. Sufficient resources

The money's in the envelope!

FREE CASH

A CASH GAME TO EXPLORE TRUST

Purpose:

1. To demonstrate how lack of trust reduces payoffs for the team

2. To explore factors that increase distrust among team members

Team Size:

9; a larger group can be divided into teams of 9. Extra participants may act as observers and advisors.

Required Resources:

1. 9 ten-dollar bills (note: You may have to spend up to $20.63 whenever you play this game)

2. 9 blank envelopes for each team

3. Calculator

Room Setup:

Push the chairs close to the walls. This game can be played with the participants standing up and walking around.

Time:

30–45 minutes

Steps:

1. **Distribute blank envelopes.** Explain that each participant is an investor. If there are more than nine participants, the others (who did not receive a blank envelope) are observers and spectators.

2. **Announce communication rules.** Investors cannot talk to one another. They cannot show or announce the amount of money they are placing inside the envelopes. Observers may talk to one another and to the investors, but they should not transmit information from one investor to another.

3. **Explain the investment procedure.** Each investor should place some money inside his or her envelope. This investment amount may vary from zero to thousands of dollars.

4. **Explain the payoff scheme.** You will count the investment money inside each envelope. This money will not be returned to the participants. If the total amount inside nine envelopes is at least $69.37, you will give each investor $10. You are not interested in individual investments, so even those who gave you empty envelopes will get $10. However, if the total investment is less than $69.37, none of the investors will get any money—not even the original investments.

5. **Announce the time limit.** Investors will have 3 minutes to make their decision, *secretly* place the investment amount inside the envelope, seal it, and write their initials on the face of the envelope. Remind the investors that they cannot communicate with one another.

6. **Audit the investments.** After a 3-minute pause, collect the envelopes. Make sure that the investor's initials are written on each envelope. Give the envelopes to one of the extra participants and ask him or her to count the money inside each envelope, leave the money inside, record the amount on the face of the envelope, and add the amounts to find the total.

7. **Ask for predictions.** While the investment amounts are being counted and added up, conduct a mini-debriefing: Ask the participants to predict the total amount and to justify their predictions. Discuss various predictions and their bases.

8. **Conclude the game.** Read the investment amounts in each envelope, without identifying the investor. Announce the total investment amount inside the envelopes. If the total is at least $69.37, give each investor $10. Keep the envelopes (with the money). If the total is less than $69.37, keep the envelopes (with the money). Explain that nobody receives $10 because the investors did not meet the minimum requirement. (You will return the investment amount later to the participants but, for the present, pretend that you are going to keep the money.)

Debriefing:

Conduct a discussion of the participants' experiences and insights. Here are some questions:

- How many of you experienced these feelings: confusion, greed, frustration, irritation, disappointment, and elation?
- If we divide the total investment requirement of $69.37 equally among the nine participants, each should invest $7.7077. How do you feel about team members who did not invest their fair share? How do you feel about team members who invested more than their fair share?

- What did you learn from participating in (or observing) the events in this simulation game?

- From your experience in playing this game, what did you learn about each of these topics: trust, teamwork, decision making, ambiguity, private versus public decisions, and personal versus team payoffs?

- Earlier participants reported that they learned the following principles. What data from the game do you have related to each of these principles?

  —Most team members want to give their fair share.

  —Some team members are greedy and some are generous.

  —Some team members don't trust other members' motivations.

  —Some team members don't trust other members' ability to divide decimal numbers and to round off the result.

  —Some team members don't trust their own mathematical abilities.

  —It is possible for a team member to make a profit of $10.

  —It is possible for the facilitator to make a profit.

  —It is difficult to make decisions about team activities without being able to talk to one another.

- In what ways does "Free Cash" remind you of team activities in the workplace?

- What would have happened if investors were permitted to talk to one another but still had to place the money *secretly* inside the envelopes?

- What would have happened if investors were given 24 hours to make up their minds?

Don't forget to include the comment of the observers during the debriefing. If time permits, facilitate a discussion on how the learning points from this game can be applied to your team. Specifically, develop a set of norms to increase the level of trust among team members.

Real team players ask for help.

HELP!

A QUICK SIMULATION ACTIVITY

Purpose:

1. To stress the importance of asking for—and offering—help in teamwork
2. To emphasize the role of managers as team leaders

Team Size:

Any number, divided into teams of 4 to 6

Required Resources:

1. Blank sheets of paper
2. Pens or pencils
3. Whistle

Time:

15–20 minutes

Room Setup:

Chairs arranged around a rectangular or round table

Steps:

1. Ask the participants to organize themselves into groups of 4 to 6.
2. In each group, ask the participants to identify the tallest member. Assign the role of manager to this person. All other participants play the role of employees. Distribute a blank sheet of paper to each employee.
3. Using your own words, give instructions such as these:

   "Managers, your task is to make sure that the employees follow my instructions and complete the task as best as possible.

   "Employees, your task is to draw a picture of a smiling face on the sheet of paper given to you. Please don't begin until I complete all my instructions. Your picture

39

should have a circular face, two dots for the eyes, and a curved line for a smiling mouth.

"One important constraint: draw the picture with your eyes closed. Please close your eyes now and keep them closed. Managers, make sure that the employees keep their eyes closed throughout this activity.

"Employees, get started. You have 30 seconds to draw your picture."

4. Pause while the employees complete the task. Blow a whistle and ask the employees to stop. Continue with these instructions:

"Employees, please keep your eyes closed. I have some more instructions for you.

"Please transfer your pen or pencil to your other hand.

"I'd like you to add a pair of ears to your picture. Don't open your eyes. Transfer your pen or pencil back to your preferred hand and draw the two ears. Please begin now.

"Managers, make sure that the employees follow my instructions."

5. Wait for the employees to complete the task. Blow the whistle.

"You may all open your eyes now. Look at your picture. Hold up your picture so the others can see it."

6. Most of the pictures are likely to have misplaced ears. Wait while the participants laugh at their efforts.

Debriefing:

The main learning point of this activity is that employees should ask for—and managers should offer—coaching and guidance. Drive home this point with questions like these:

"Most of us know the importance of asking for coaching help. How many of you asked your manager for guidance while drawing your picture?"

Congratulate employees who asked for coaching. Ask them to hold up their pictures. Continue with the debriefing, borrowing from this suggested script:

"Some of you may feel that the manager's role is to supervise and control. Change your perception from being employees and managers to being team members and leaders. In a team you should ask for help from everybody including the team leader. And if you are the leader you should offer help to all members of the team.

"If you are an employee, ask for help. If you are a manager, offer help. Don't wait until it's too late. "

Variation:

End the activity on a positive note by asking the employees to close their eyes and add a nose to the picture. Remind the employees to ask for help and the managers to give appropriate help.

Here's a great discussion starter on team member recognition.

HOW DO YOU LIKE YOUR RECOGNITON?

A SELF-ASSESSMENT

Purpose:

1. To give team members an opportunity to understand what types of recognition they value

2. To give team members an opportunity to learn what motivates their teammates

3. To help team members and others tailor their recognition more specifically to the needs of their teammates

Team Size:

Most useful as an exercise for an intact team of 10 or less. However, it can be used in a team-training class of 20 to 30 people. It can even be adapted for use with larger groups that are divided into small sub-groups.

Required Resources:

1. A copy of "How Do You Like Your Recognition?" for each person (p. 43)
2. A copy of "How Do You Like Your Recognition?" score sheet for each person (p. 44)

Time:

1 hour

Room Setup:

Chairs around a rectangular or round table for an intact team; for a large group, clusters of chairs and tables set around the room

Steps:

1. Explain the purpose of the activity.

2. Distribute the "How Do You Like Your Recognition?" handout to each person. Ask each person to complete the survey individually.

3. Distribute the score sheet and ask each person to compete the form.

4. Present a lecturette on the difference between intrinsic and extrinsic motivation. Explain that *extrinsic motivators* are forms of recognition that come from outside the person and appeal to the outer-directed self. *Intrinsic motivators* appeal to the inner self because they focus on things that may be apparent only to that person. Both motivators have their place, and one is not better than the other. You may want to refer to a basic psychology text for more background on motivation before doing this session.

5. With an intact team ask each person to share his or her results and talk more specifically about what motivates and what de-motivates him or her, why certain things would be especially appealing while others would be a real turn-off, and, if possible, to share some examples of recognition each has received in the past (and how each person reacted to it).

Debriefing:

Facilitate a close to this activity by asking what people learned and how they can use it.

- What did you learn about recognition?
- What did you learn about yourself?
- What did you learn about your teammates?
- How will you use your new knowledge in the future?
- How will it help increase team effectiveness?

Variation:

1. It may be fun and useful to obtain a team score for extrinsic and intrinsic motivators. Add all the scores for each and divide by the number of participants to get a team average for intrinsic and extrinsic forms of recognition. Use these results as a basis for a discussion on forms of recognition for the team as a whole.

2. If time is short, ask people to fill out the survey as pre-work for the session.

HOW DO YOU LIKE YOUR RECOGNITION?

Directions: Please review the following list of forms of recognition. Check the forms that you would value and like to receive. You may check as many as you like, but check only the ones that appeal to you.

_____ 1. Receive positive verbal feedback at a staff meeting.

_____ 2. Asked to take on a tough problem or new challenge.

_____ 3. Asked to give a presentation on your work at a staff meeting or a company conference.

_____ 4. Receive positive, handwritten comments in the margin of a document you prepared.

_____ 5. Invited to a barbecue or dinner party at the home of your boss.

_____ 6. Given the opportunity to work flexible hours or work at home.

_____ 7. Go to a golf and tennis weekend at a beautiful resort with other award winners from the organization.

_____ 8. Given the opportunity to purchase new tools and equipment to enhance your work.

_____ 9. Have your picture and a story about your work appear in the company or community newspaper.

_____ 10. Asked for your opinion on a difficult organizational problem or a new business opportunity.

_____ 11. Given the opportunity to speak about your work at an important professional conference.

_____ 12. Offered the opportunity to learn a new system, operate some new equipment, or in other ways increase your skills and knowledge.

_____ 13. In a prominent location, have your picture displayed along with either letters of commendation or a description of your work or both.

_____ 14. Asked to help a colleague get started with a project or solve a particularly difficult problem.

_____ 15. Receive verbal recognition for your work from a senior-level executive at a company forum attended by you and your colleagues.

_____ 16. A solution that you recommended is being implemented throughout the organization.

_____ 17. A customer or other stakeholder sends a letter to your boss praising your work.

_____ 18. When you ask for help, your boss offers to pick up some of the load directly, share his or her expertise, or obtain outside assistance.

_____ 19. Receive a T-shirt, hat, or mug with your name or other indication on it that makes it clear that it is recognition for your work.

_____ 20. Empowered to make decisions or act in other ways that increase control over your work.

HOW DO YOU LIKE YOUR RECOGNITION?

SCORE SHEET

Directions: Please transfer your responses to the columns below. Place a check in the blanks that you checked on the survey and then tally the columns.

Extrinsic	Intrinsic
1. _____	2. _____
3. _____	4. _____
5. _____	6. _____
7. _____	8. _____
9. _____	10. _____
11. _____	12. _____
13. _____	14. _____
15. _____	16. _____
17. _____	18. _____
19 . _____	20. _____
TOTAL = _____	TOTAL = _____

Here's an activity for geographically dispersed teams.

METCALFE

A LARGE GROUP TEAM-BUILDING ACTIVITY

Purpose:

1. To explore factors that increase the value of a communication network

2. To understand the importance of influencing others to join a communications network

3. To explore the differences between electronic and face-to-face communication for virtual teams

Team Size:

At least 10. The activity is more exciting with a large number of participants. We have played METCALFE with groups of 200!

Required Resources:

1. A question grid for each participant. This is a 5 x 5 grid with 25 questions. (See page 48 for a sample with questions about science fiction authors.) You can reproduce this sample or create your own grids with questions on locally relevant topics. However, choose questions that are unlikely to be answered by the participants.

   Insert the correct answers for a few squares in each grid, using the answers on page 49 or your own answers. The number of these answers depends on the number of participants. For example, if you have 25 participants, each grid has only one correct answer. With fewer participants, include more answers in each grid. Distribute the answers among the grids in such a way that the complete set of grids contains all the answers and no two grids have the same answers.

   Each grid also specifies a wait time. Randomly use 2 or 3 minutes as the wait time among different grids.

2. An index card, a poker chip, or some other small item to represent the WTE (whose function is described below)

3. Timer

4. Whistle

Time:

30 minutes

Room Setup:

Push all chairs against the wall. Participants will be standing up and walking around throughout the activity.

Steps:

1. **Distribute a question grid to each participant.** Ask the participant to study the grid and note that it includes one or more answers. Also call attention to the wait-time line. Point out that different participants have different answers and wait-time specifications.

2. **Brief the players.** Explain that participants win if they collect and write down the correct answers for all five questions in any row or column of the grid. Participants may share only the pre-printed answers from their grid with others. They may not share answers collected from other participants.

3. **Explain the communication procedure.** Strict rules control the communication procedure. All exchanges of answers take place on a one-on-one basis. During this transaction, one participant (the initiator) approaches another and says, "I want to talk to you." The other participant (the responder) says, "Okay" and begins timing using a watch. The two participants may not talk until the responder's wait time has expired. At this time, they exchange the pre-printed answer (or answers) with each other.

4. **Announce the availability of WTE.** Participants may purchase a special device called a wait time eliminator (WTE) from the facilitator for 25 cents. If both the initiator and the responder have WTEs, they do not have to wait before sharing their answers. However, if only one of the two participants has a WTE, both participants have to wait. A participant may collect WTEs and give them to other participants. However, he or she may not take back the WTE after the exchange of answers.

5. **Explain the whisper and shout rules.** The exchange of answers between two participants takes place in a whisper to prevent others from overhearing. However, any participant may shout general procedural suggestions to the whole group at any time.

6. **Conduct the activity.** Blow the whistle and announce the official start of the activity. Start the timer and monitor participant behaviors. Sell WTEs to any participant who gives you 25 cents. Remind the buyer that the WTEs work only if both participants have them.

7. **Conclude the session.** If a participant brings a question grid with the correct answers to five questions in a column or a row, quickly check the answers and congratulate him or her. However, continue with the activity and identify the subsequent winners who complete the task within the allotted time. At the end of 10 minutes, blow the whistle and announce the end of the session.

Debriefing:

1. **Explain the metaphor.** Tell participants that the activity simulates the functioning of a network and a WTE represents such telecommunications devices as telephones, pagers, videophones, fax machines, and e-mail systems. The wait time symbolizes the time lost while arranging for a convenient meeting date and time. The main point of the activity is the elimination of the wait time through the use of electronic communications devices.

2. **Explain Metcalfe's Law.** Robert Metcalfe, founder of 3Com Corporation, points out that the value of a network rapidly increases as more people join it. For example, if you are the only person on earth with a fax machine, it is of no use. However, if everyone has a fax machine, then its usefulness becomes immense, permitting instant communication (if only we can control the spam, the electronic equivalent of junk mail).

3. **Discuss the activity.** Here are some suggested questions:

   - How does this activity reflect Metcalfe's Law?

   - How has Metcalfe's Law affected your interactions? Do you have e-mail access? Has its usefulness increased over the years as more and more of your friends and clients have access to it?

   - How does Metcalfe's Law affect interaction among team members who are geo-graphically dispersed?

   - If we want to simulate electronic forums, list-serves, and chat rooms, how should we modify this activity?

   - What are the major advantages and disadvantages of expanding electronic net-works?

Variations:

1. Distribute a few free WTEs to participants near the beginning of the activity.

2. Assign the role of high-tech entrepreneurs to few participants. These participants do not receive question grids. Instead, they sell WTEs to other participants.

QUESTION GRID
(Wait Time: _____ Minutes)

1. How many Hugos did Robert Heinlein win? _____	2. Has Robert Heinlein won the Grand Master Nebula? _____	3. What is Isaac Asimov's most recent novel? _____	4. Is Ray Bradbury still alive? _____	5. In what year was Ursula K. LeGuin born? _____
6. What is Ray Bradbury's most recent novel? _____	7. What is Robert Heinlein's most recent novel? _____	8. Has Arthur C. Clarke won the Grand Master Nebula? _____	9. Has Ursula K. LeGuin won the Grand Master Nebula? _____	10. In what year was Robert Heinlein born? _____
11. Is Isaac Asimov still alive? _____	12. In what year was Isaac Asimov born? _____	13. What is Ursula K. LeGuin's most recent novel? _____	14. What is Arthur C. Clarke's most recent novel? _____	15. How many Hugos did Arthur C. Clarke win? _____
16. Is Arthur C. Clarke still alive? _____	17. In what year was Ray Bradbury born? _____	18. In what year was Arthur C. Clarke born? _____	19. Is Ursula K. LeGuin still alive? _____	20. Is Robert Heinlein still alive? _____
21. How many Hugos did Isaac Asimov win? _____	22. How many Hugos did Ursula K. LeGuin win? _____	23. How many Hugos did Ray Bradbury win? _____	24. Has Isaac Asimov won the Grand Master Nebula? _____	25. Has Ray Bradbury won the Grand Master Nebula? _____

ANSWERS

1. How many Hugos did Robert Heinlein win? FOUR	2. Has Robert Heinlein won the Grand Master Nebula? YES	3. Isaac Asimov: FORWARD THE FOUNTAIN	4. Is Ray Bradbury still alive? YES	5. In what year was Ursula K. LeGuin born? 1929
6. Ray Bradbury: GREEN SHADOWS, WHITE WHALE	7. Robert Heinlein: TO SAIL BEYOND THE SUNSET	8. Has Arthur C. Clarke won the Grand Master Nebula? YES	9. Has Ursula K. LeGuin won the Grand Master Nebula? NO	10. In what year was Robert Heinlein born? 1907
11. Is Isaac Asimov stil alive? NO	12. In what year was Isaac Asimov born? 1920	13. Ursula K. LeGuin: TEHANU: THE LAST BOOK OF EARTHSEA	14. Arthur C. Clarke: 3001: THE FINAL ODESSEY	15. How many Hugos did Arthur C. Clarke win? THREE
16. Is Arthur C. Clarke still alive? YES	17. In what year was Ray Bradbury born? 1920	18. In what year was Arthur C. Clarke born? 1917	19. Is Ursula K. LeGuin still alive? YES	20. Is Robert Heinlein still alive? NO
21. How many Hugos did Isaac Asimov win? SEVEN	22. How many Hugos did Ursula K. LeGuin win? FIVE	23. How many Hugos did Ray Bradbury win? NONE	24. Has Isaac Asimov won the Grand Master Nebula? YES	25. Has Ray Bradbury won the Grand Master Nebula? YES

An activity for soap-opera fans.

OUR TEAM
LEARNING THE STAGES OF TEAM DEVELOPMENT

Purpose:

1. To identify the stages in the development of a team
2. To personalize the team-development stages by incorporating them in a fictional case study

Team Size:

Any number can play. This activity works best with 12 to 30 participants.

Required Resources:

Copies of the handout, "Stages in Team Development" from page 53

Time:

45 minutes

Room Setup:

Chairs arranged around a rectangular or round table

Preparation:

1. **Master the model.** Your success in this activity will depend on your familiarity with the team-development model. Carefully study the model in the handout, and figure out what is happening in each step and how the steps are linked.

2. **Create a case study.** Make up a story that illustrates the application of the team-development process. This is what you will be asking the participants to do, and you need a sample. You can base your story on one of your own successful projects. If you do so, don't let facts get in the way of a good story that clearly tracks the team's growth through the stages. If you are adventurous, create a story around a popular TV show.

Steps:

1. **Brief the participants.** Using your own words, introduce the team-development model.
   - Bruce W. Tuckman suggested that all teams go through four distinctive stages in their development.
   - The basic model has been in use with minor adaptations for the past four decades.
   - The model has important implications for organizing, building, and managing a team.

2. **Distribute the handout that explains the model.** Point out that the handout identifies the stages in the development of a team and the relationships among the stages. Ask participants to read and review the handout. Announce a 3-minute time limit for this activity.

3. **Tell your story.** At the end of the time limit, announce that you are going to tell the story of a team to make the abstract model become concrete. Narrate your story, pausing at the end of each section to relate it to the stages in the team-development process.

4. **Distribute the case study.** Explain that this case study illustrates the stages in team development. Suggest that the participants refer to this case study later—after you give them an assignment.

5. **Assign the story-creation task.** Divide the participants into teams of three to five members each. Ask each team to create a story to illustrate the team-development model. The story may be based on a team member's experience, or a historical event, or some popular TV show. The story should clearly illustrate the different stages. Teams have 11 minutes to create the story.

6. **Conduct a storytelling session.** Give the teams a 1-minute warning. Ask the teams to give finishing touches to the story and to select a representative to present it to the whole group. After another minute, randomly choose a team to send its story-teller to the front of the room. Ask this person to present the story. At the conclusion of the story, select another team. Repeat the process until all teams have presented their stories.

7. **Conclude with a *caveat*.** Briefly comment on the stories, and congratulate the teams on their depth of understanding of the team-development process. In your own words, explain the advantages of mastering this team-development model:

   - The model enables us to anticipate what a team is likely to go through. This will prevent team members from being surprised or depressed by various events such as increasing disagreements during the storming stage.
   - The model enables us to use appropriate strategies to smooth the progress of a team through the different stages. For example, we can suggest a procedure for establishing ground rules to a team in the norming stage.
   - The model suggests suitable leadership and membership behaviors during each stage of a team's development.

However, point out the inherent danger in mindlessly assuming a linear stage-by-stage development of a team:

- Different teams may proceed through different stages at different speeds. Members of a team should avoid making self-fulfilling prophecies about how long each stage will last.

- A team may sometimes regress to an earlier stage. For example, team members may return to a previous stage if they discover that the team's mission or membership has changed.

- It is possible for a team to be in different stages with respect to different aspects of its mission. For example, it may still be storming about implementing its final plan even while it is performing efficiently in generating ideas for the plan.

Debriefing:

Conduct a discussion session to reflect on participants' experiences. Here are some suggested questions:

- Think of the different teams that you belong to. What is the current stage of development for each team? What does each need to do to move to the next stage?

- Can you recall examples of behaviors that belong to different stages in the development of a team to which you currently belong?

- How do you think the four stages will play out when we create a virtual team through the Internet?

Variations:

1. Have the teams act out their stories as skits.

2. After all teams have presented their stories, ask the participants to vote for the Most Outstanding Story Award.

STAGES IN TEAM DEVELOPMENT

Bruce W. Tuckman and several other psychologists who study the behavior of small groups suggest that all teams go through four distinct stages in their development.

1. The first stage in a team's development is forming. During this stage, team members are unsure about what they are doing. Their focus is on understanding the team's goal and its role. Team members worry about whether the other team members will accept them, and they frequently look for clarification from their leader.

2. The second stage in a team's development is storming. During this stage, the team members try to get their act together. This stage is marked by conflict among the members and between the members and the leader. Through this conflict, the team attempts to define itself.

3. The third stage in a team's development is norming. This stage follows storming, after the team members succeed in resolving their conflicts. They now feel more secure with one another and with their leader. They effectively negotiate the structure of the team, the division of labor, and norms regarding such issues as decision making, communications, and leadership.

4. The fourth stage in a team's development is performing. During this stage, the team members behave in a mature fashion and focus on accomplishing their goals. This stage is marked by direct, two-way communication among team members and by equal focus on getting the work done and maintaining the team.

Can you elaborate on a quote for 30 seconds?

QUOTES FROM EXPERTS
AN INTER-TEAM CONTEST

Purpose:
1. To explore essential elements of teamwork by reflecting on quotes and identifying their relevance
2. To reflect on the teamwork that involved in preparing and making a presentation

Team Size:
Any number of participants, divided into teams of 3 to 7 members each

Required Resources:
Quote cards. Make photocopies of quotes from experts (p. 56) on card stock. Make two copies of each page and cut the individual cards. You should have pairs of cards for each quote.

Time:
30–45 minutes; the exact time depends on the number of teams

Room Setup:
Chairs around rectangular or round tables

Steps:
1. Organize participants into teams of 3 to 7 members each. Select as many quote cards as there are teams. Distribute the cards in such a way that each team gets two different quotes and each quote is given to two different teams.
2. Ask the teams to reflect on each quote, discover its deeper meaning, and identify its relevance to effective teamwork. Warn the teams that they will be asked to make a 30-second presentation on each quote they received. Announce a suitable time limit of 10–15 minutes. Start the timer.

3. Pause while the teams work on analyzing the quotes and preparing their presentations. Remind the teams that they should work on both quotes.

4. Announce a 1-minute warning. A minute later, blow the whistle to signal the end of the preparation time.

5. Read one of the quotes (or display it on the screen). Ask the members of the two teams that worked on this quote to stand up. Send one team out of the room.

6. Ask the other team to make its presentation. Cut it off after 30 seconds if the team does not stop. Call the other to the room and have its spokesperson make the presentation.

7. After the two presentations, invite comments from the audience. If appropriate, ask the audience to vote (by their applause) to identify the better presentation.

8. Repeat the same procedure with the other quotes.

Debriefing:

Explain to participants that, although the content of the quotes have been thoroughly discussed, you would like to spend some time discussing the process by which teams developed their presentations. Use these suggested questions for debriefing:

- Did all members of the team contribute to the design of the presentation?

- Did the team members play different roles in the analysis of the quote and the preparation of the presentation? If so, what were the different roles?

- How did the team handle the two different quotes: both at the same time or one after the other? Did any team divide themselves into sub-teams for handling the two quotes? How satisfied were you with the way you managed the time?

- How did you select the team member (or members) to make the presentation?

- How do the quotes that you heard apply to your teamwork in preparing and making the presentation?

Variation:

Use "Quotes from Experts" as a closing activity. Encourage the teams to relate the quotes to the new principles and procedures they learned earlier.

Everyone is needed, but no one is necessary.

Bruce Coslet

The ratio of We's to I's is the best indicator of the development of a team.

Lewis B. Eigen

The needs of the team are best met when we meet the needs of individual persons.

Max Depree

Do you want a collection of brilliant minds or a brilliant collection of minds?

R. Meredith

Teams share the burden and divide the grief.

Doug Smith

The strength of the team is each individual member. . . . The strength of each member is the team.

Phil Jackson

Team members who feel threatened but who are not aware of it become rigid—and that stops teamwork.

Will Schultz

A team is more than a collection of people. It is a process of give and take.

Barbara Clacel and Emile Robert, Jr.

Talent wins games, but teamwork wins championships.

Michael Jordan

None of us is a smart as all of us.

Ken Blanchard

Here's a simulation designed specifically for a geographically dispersed team.

REAL VIRTUAL

A SIMULATION GAME

Purpose:

1. To examine the barriers to trust in a virtual team

2. To help a virtual or geographically dispersed team develop effective communication and trust

3. To highlight the importance of both task and process in a team

Team Size:

The minimum number of participants for this game is 9. As the number of participants increases, both the number of teams and the membership of each team can increase. Ideally, the number of teams should be 5, and the maximum membership in each team should not exceed 5 as well.

Required Resources:

1. Role cards for all participants. You will need an equal number of task role cards and relationship role cards (see p. 60). Copy the role descriptions on 3 × 5 cards.

2. "Observer/Transmitter Guide" for 1 person in each team (p. 61)

3. "Team Observer Sheet" for 1 person in each team (p. 62)

4. Bulletin board or similar board for the posting of notes

5. Large Post-it Notes™ pad for each team

6. 3 × 5 cards for each team

7. Pens

8. A business-size envelope for each team

9. Quote divided into chunks as provided in handout (p. 63). Cut up chunks and place at least 2 chunks in each envelope. You will need 1 envelope for each team.

10. "Directions for Solving a Chunks Puzzle" for each team (p. 64)

11. "Blank Chunks Puzzle Sheet" for each team (p. 65)

12. "Team Debriefing Guide" (p. 66)

Time:

60 to 90 minutes

Room Setup:

One large room with tables and chairs set in a U-shape or seminar style for the entire group. A break-out room for each team. The bulletin board should be hung in the large room or in a common area.

Steps:

1. Explain that the purpose of the simulation is to create a situation in which the only way the members can communicate with one another is by e-mail, fax, or posting a message on a common electronic bulletin board. In this exercise, we will not use computers but rather will simulate these various forms of communication. The key factor is that there will be no face-to-face interaction.

2. Divide into at least three teams. Ask one person on each team to be the Observer/Transmitter. Give each person the Guide and the Sheet (see #2 and #3 under Required Resources) and ask him or her to spend a few minutes studying them; however, these people may not show them to their team members.

3. Give each team an envelope with chunks, a "Blank Chunks Puzzle Sheet," and the "Directions for Solving a Chunks Puzzle." Spend a few minutes clarifying the task. It should be made clear that each team has some of the clues to the Chunks puzzle and that the entire team must work together to solve it. Participants may share their information only via e-mail, fax, and the electronic bulletin board.

4. Distribute the role cards in such a way that half of each team receives task role cards and half receives relationship role cards. Participants are not to share their cards with their team members. Give them a few minutes to think about how they will carry out their role in the context of both the task and the communications tools available to them. Distribute the Post-it Notes. Clarify that they are to be used for posting messages on the electronic bulletin board.

5. Show everyone where the electronic bulletin board is located. Clarify that this is the one place where a message can be posted for reading by all team members. However, only your Observer/Transmitter can come to the area to post and read messages. The Observers/Transmitters are free to write down posted messages and bring them to the teams.

6. Send each team to its assigned break-out room. Make it clear that from this point on there will be no face-to-face communication with members of the other teams.

7. Allow 30 minutes for the team to solve the Chunks puzzle.

8. Ask each team to conduct a self-assessment of the activity using the Debriefing Guide.

9. Then ask the Observers/Transmitters to provide their feedback.

Debriefing:

Bring all the teams back together for a final debriefing using some or all of these questions:

- What are some of the things that your team did to complete this assignment?
- How did you address the conflicts between members?
- What are some of the things that you did to work with the other teams? Did you have a plan or did you follow certain tactics?
- What helped to build trust with the other groups?
- What were some of the barriers to building trust with the other groups?
- How did the lack of face-to-face contact help or hinder the process?
- If you believe a face-to-face meeting would have helped, when should the meeting have occurred and what should have been discussed?
- What are some of the lessons, or takeaways, from this simulation?
- How will you apply some of what you learned to your back-home situation?

Variations:

Instead of asking teams to solve the Chunks puzzle, use an open-ended business problem that does not have a "right" answer.

ROLE DESCRIPTIONS

Task Role Description:

Your primary focus is on solving the Chunks puzzle and completing this project on time. While you know that building good relationships is important to the successful completion of a project, you believe that time limitations and the complexity of the task mean that the team can't do anything except "get the job done." Do what you can to carry out this role, and stay in your role throughout the activity. Do not show your card to your teammates.

Relationship Role Description:

Your primary focus is on building trusting relationships with team members in other locations. While you know that each team will be judged primarily on how quickly and correctly it completes the assignment, you believe that people will not share information and work together unless they get to know and trust one another first. Do what you can to carry out your role, and stay in your role throughout the activity. Do not show your card to your teammates.

OBSERVER/TRANSMITTER GUIDE

Role: You have two roles. First, to observe the internal dynamics of your team and provide feedback on the process and, second, to take e-mail and fax messages to the other teams and to post notes on and bring notes from the electronic bulletin board.

Rules:

1. Do not participate in your team's discussion in any manner. You are a silent observer.

2. When you deliver messages to the other teams, do not talk to any member of the teams.

3. Your communication with your group is limited to clarifying to which team their message is to be delivered.

4. When you post or pick up messages from the bulletin board, you should not communicate with other observers/transmitters.

5. When you are not transmitting messages, stay with your team and observe the process. Use the Observer Sheet.

6. Sit with the team when they debrief the activity, but do not actively participate in the discussions. State your opinion if they request it. However, you want to let them conduct their self-assessment before you provide your observations.

7. Provide your feedback based on the Observer Sheet.

TEAM OBSERVER SHEET

Directions: Always sit outside the group but in a position where you can see and hear most of the discussion. **Take notes, especially comments that helped or hindered the process.** You are looking for behaviors that helped get the task done, built positive relationships in the team, developed cooperative relations with the other groups, enhanced communication, and established trust.

1. **Planning.** Did the group take some time to clarify the task, establish a process, clarify roles and other planning activities before jumping in to solving the Chunks puzzle? What specifically did they do?

2. **Task-Focused Behaviors.** What things did team members do that helped or hindered getting the assignment completed?

3. **Relationship-Building Behaviors.** What things did team members do that helped or hindered their ability to work together in their team?

4. **Inter-Group Teaming.** What things did the team do that helped or hindered cooperation with the other teams?

5. **Your Role.** How did you feel about your role? Did you ever want to do more than you were asked to do? Did you feel constrained by the rules?

CHUNKS PUZZLE

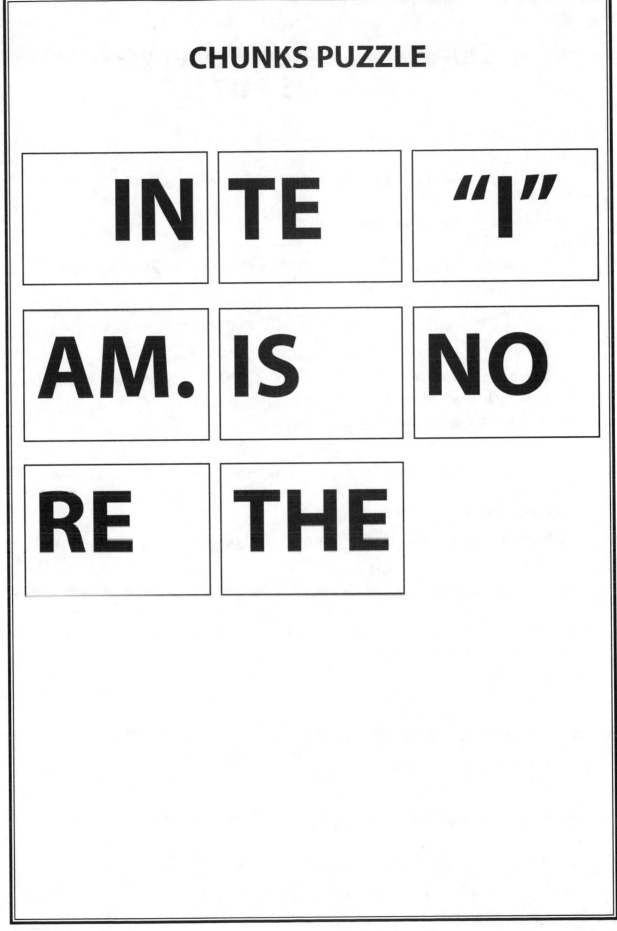

IN	TE	"I"
AM.	IS	NO
RE	THE	

DIRECTIONS FOR SOLVING
A CHUNKS PUZZLE

We took a sentence and cut it up into three-character chunks including spaces and punctuation marks.

The task of your team is to rearrange the chunks to form the original sentence.

Each team has been given some chunks. The team has to work together to solve the puzzle.

Hints:

- The sentence is about an important principle of teamwork.

- Locate the chunk that contains a period. This should be the last chunk. Try working backward from this chunk.

- Any chunk that begins with a space is the beginning of a new word. Look for other chunks that could follow this chunk.

- If you have discovered a chunk that looks like the beginning of a word (but does not have a space in front), this could be the first word in the sentence.

- Print the chunks on the blank Chunks puzzle sheet to show the original sentence.

BLANK CHUNKS PUZZLE SHEET

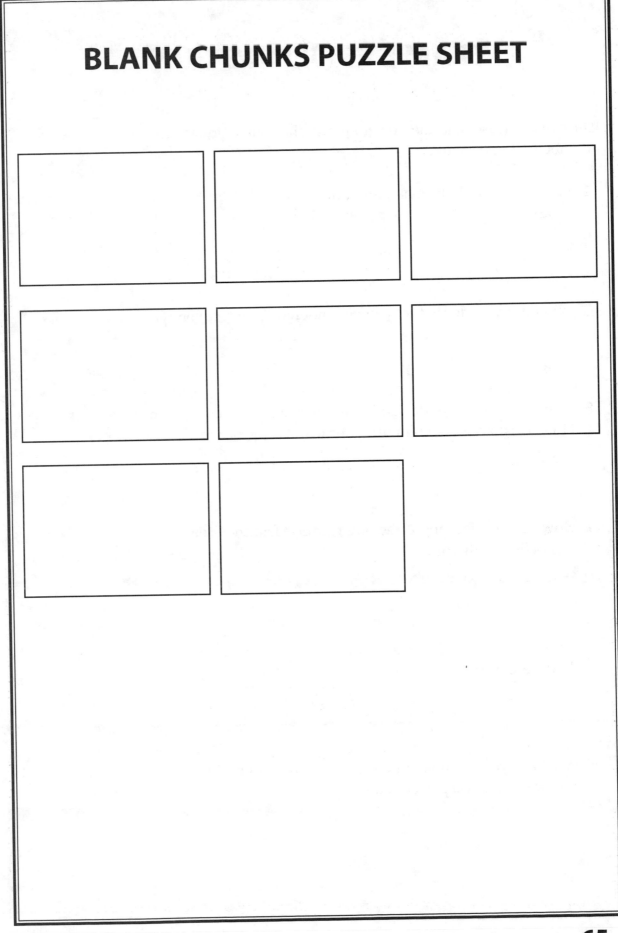

TEAM DEBRIEFING GUIDE

Directions: Please read the questions and then share your reactions with the other members of your team.

1. What did you do that helped your team work more effectively with the other groups?

2. What did you do that may have hindered the effectiveness of your team?

3. How did your team decide on its approach to working with the other teams? How satisfied were you with your team's approach?

4. How did you feel about the other teams? Did they seem to be cooperating or competing with you?

5. If you were given the opportunity to do this project again, what would you do differently?

6. What did you learn about communication and problem solving among geographically dispersed teams?

Here's a structure to encourage team learning.

SDLT

A Self-Directed Learning Team Activity

Purpose:

1. To structure mutual learning in an intact team
2. To share and analyze team members' experiences, knowledge, and opinions

Team Size:

Works best with a team of 12–20 participants

Required Resources:

1. A handout summarizing the TOP TIPS procedure (for a sample, see page 70). Reproduce 1 copy for each participant.
2. A timer and a whistle to help you stick to the schedule

Time:

45 minutes (depends on the number of topics and the amount of time allotted to each round)

Room Setup:

Move all chairs to the wall (team members stand up and move around during this activity)

Preparation:

Select a task commonly performed by team members. Identify 4–6 topics related to this task. Prepare a handout similar to the sample on page 70. Replace the task and the topics in the sample handout with your content. Make any other changes to suit your needs. For example, in a recent meeting, we conducted an SDLT session on the task of handling disruptive team members. Our list of topics included domination, lack of participation, excessive seriousness, flippancy, side conversations, and emotional outbursts.

Steps:

1. **Work individually on the first topic.** Announce the topic and assign a suitable time limit. Ask each team member to recall successful strategies that she or he has used in this area. Also invite participants to recall tips and short cuts that they have heard about or read about. Recommend that the participants jot down notes for personal use.

2. **Work with a partner.** After a suitable pause, blow a whistle and ask each team member to find a partner to share tips with. Warn the partners that they will have to recall and present the other person's tips at a later time. Encourage participants to listen carefully and take notes. If there is an odd number of team members, ask the extra person to join a pair to form a triad.

3. **Work in quads.** After a suitable pause to permit the sharing of tips between partners, blow the whistle again and ask each pair to join another pair to form a group of four, called a *quad*. (If there is an odd number, three of the pairs may join one another to form a group of six.) Ask all four members of each quad to share the tips from the previous round, each person recalling and reporting her or his partner's tips.

4. **Select the best tips.** Blow the whistle again and ask each quad to select two or three of their tips for presentation to the entire team. Recommend that the participants select practical tips that are unique.

5. **Present to the whole group.** Blow the whistle again and randomly select one of the quads. Ask the spokesperson from this quad to present its best tip. Repeat the procedure with a few other quads.

6. **Repeat the procedure.** Announce the next topic. Take the team members through the steps of individual-, partner-, quad-, and whole-group presentation as before. Repeat the same procedure with the remaining topics.

Debriefing:

Ask each participant to take a few minutes to recall the different tips and to jot down personal notes about two or three of them for immediate application in his or her workplace.

- Discuss the activity with the participants. Here are some suggested questions: What are some common themes emerging among different tips?
- What was the most useful tip for each topic?
- Did you contribute your fair share of tips? If not, why not?
- What are the advantages and disadvantages of openly sharing tips among team members?
- What other methods will permit us to share such tips among the team members?

Variations:

1. Speed up the activity by reducing the number of topics, reducing the time allotted to each round, asking the participants to work in pairs from the beginning, and skipping the formation of quads.

2. Ask the team members to specify the topics at the beginning of the activity.

SDLT

How to Participate

The Self-Directed Learning Team (SDLT) activity is designed to help us share practical tips, ideas, and strategies related to a common task.

Today's task is *Handling Disruptive Participants in Team Meetings*

These are the six specific topics that we will explore:

1. Domination: How do we handle people who talk too much and interrupt the others?

2. Lack of participation: How do we handle people who are totally withdrawn and do not want to participate in the meeting?

3. Excessive seriousness: How do we handle people who are uptight about everything and always talk in a politically correct fashion?

4. Flippancy: How do we handle people who use excessive humor and make fun of the important issues?

5. Side conversations: How do we handle people who whisper or pass notes to each other and conduct a separate discussion?

6. Emotional outbursts: How do we handle people who lose their temper, attack each other, or get excessively emotional?

Procedure

To ensure that everyone gets maximum benefit from this activity, we will use the following procedure:

1. **Work by yourself.** Recall successful short-cut strategies that you have used in this task. Also recall tips and short cuts that you have heard about or read about. Jot down notes for personal reference.

2. **Work with a partner.** Find a partner and share your tips and short-cut strategies. Listen carefully, because you will have to recall and present your partner's tips to the others.

3. **Work in quads.** Join another pair to form a team of four called a *quad*. Share the tips from the previous round, each person recalling and reporting her or his partner's tips.

4. **Work with the whole group.** Select the best tips from your quad. Make a brief presentation of the one best tip. Listen to the tips presented by the other quads.

Repeat the same procedure with each of the six topics. At the end of the session make a note of two or three strategies that you want to apply.

This brief activity requires people to confront some practical, day-to-day problems.

SITUATION ANALYSIS
A PROBLEM-SOLVING ACTIVITY

Purpose:
1. To develop methods of dealing with typical team issues
2. To practice problem solving in a team setting
3. To examine process issues in team problem solving

Team Size:
This activity is designed for small groups of 4 to 6 participants each

Required Resources:
1. Sufficient copies of the handout "Situation Analysis" cases 1–4, pp. 73–76
2. Flip chart, pad, markers, and masking tape

Time:
45 minutes to 1 hour; however, if time is limited, give each team only one case to solve

Room Setup:
Chairs in a circle or set around a round or rectangular table for each team; flip chart up front

Steps:
1. Review the cases for relevance to your organization. Edit as appropriate and/or add other situations.
2. Explain the purpose of the activity.
3. Distribute the situations. Allow 10 minutes per case. Ask each group to select a spokesperson to present their recommendations.

4. Facilitate a discussion as the reports are presented, asking for reactions from the other teams. Probe if you feel that the team has not sufficiently looked at the hard issues associated with each case.

Debriefing:

Conclude the activity by facilitating a discussion on what has been learned from the cases and their applications to your "back home" situation. Here are some possible questions.

- What did you learn about being an effective team member?
- What types of things help a team deal with all the issues in these cases?
- How are these situations different from or similar to your team's issues?
- As a result of this activity, what new behaviors would you add to your list of team norms?

Variations:

1. Add some fun and some competition to the activity by asking everyone to vote for the team that did the best, most thoughtful analysis of their situation. People cannot, however, vote for *their* team. Collect the ballots and tally the result; have some prizes for the winning team. Be sure to announce the competition *before* the teams go to work on the task.

2. Enhance the learning by assigning process observers to each team. Ask the observers to report at the end of step 3, *before* each team presents its recommendations. Use the Observer Guide from "Sleepless in Seattle" (p. 81).

3. Instead of, or in addition to, using the observers, ask each team to conduct a self-assessment of its process. Use the Process Review from "Escape from Gilligan's Island" (p. 30).

SITUATION ANALYSIS

Case #1: Critical Cross-Functional Team Problem

You notice that another team member is pulling less than a full share of the team's load.

- If you were the team leader, what would you do?

- If you were another team member, what would you do?

SITUATION ANALYSIS

Case #2: Team-Meeting Time Robbers

You are running a team meeting. A lot of time seems to be wasted because of irrelevant conversation.

- What should you do right now?

- What should you do in the future?

SITUATION ANALYSIS

Case #3: Personal Priority Setting

You are a member of a part-time product development team that is working on an important new product. However, you also have other responsibilities associated with the ongoing work of your department.

You must set priorities to help you decide what to work on first.

- What questions would help you set these priorities?

SITUATION ANALYSIS

Case #4: Gaining Acceptance

Your team has developed a plan for making some dramatic improvements in customer service. However, the plan involves some significant initial cost associated with new systems as well as a restructuring of the customer service function.

Your senior management sponsor has never opposed anything the team has done in the past but has not shown any great interest either.

- How should the team approach her now?

- What should be the team's long-term strategy with her?

Here's a fun way to demonstrate the challenges and opportunities of cross-team collaboration.

SLEEPLESS IN SEATTLE

AN INTER-GROUP TEAM GAME

Purpose:

1. To demonstrate the barriers to teamwork between departments in an organization
2. To experience the inherent competition between groups that can block collaboration
3. To develop strategies for improving inter-group teamwork in an organization

Team Size:

The minimum size group is 12; however, the preferred size is 16. The activity can be run comfortably with up to 25 to 30 people.

Required Resources:

1. A set of cards printed on card stock. If you have 12 to 16 participants you will use cards from only 3 of the cities (e. g., "Sleepless in Seattle," "Fearless in Philly," and "Aimless in Atlanta") (p. 80). If your group is larger, you can add cities to the game.
2. A "Process Observer" handout for each group (p. 81)
3. Flip chart, pad, markers, masking tape or push pins

Time:

60 to 90 minutes

Room Setup:

Clusters of chairs or chairs around small tables set around the room so that each group can have private conversations; 1 table at the front of the room for the facilitator

Steps:

1. Form sub-groups of 4 to 5 members. Label each group by one of the city names (e. g., "Clueless in Chicago"). Write the group name on a sheet of flip-chart paper and post it on the wall next to the group's location. Ask for 1 volunteer from each group to serve as observer. Give them the Process Observer handout.

77

2. Before the session, mix up the cards of the cities chosen for the game. Give each group a mix of cards from all the selected cities. In addition, give each one a different number of cards. Place each team's cards in an envelope. For example, if you are playing the game with three cities—Seattle, Atlanta, and Chicago—divide the cards as follows:

—"Sleepless in Seattle" Group: 2 Seattle cards, 2 Atlanta cards, and 3 Chicago cards

—"Aimless in Atlanta" Team: 1 Atlanta card, 1 Chicago card, and 2 Seattle cards

—"Clueless in Chicago" Team: 2 Chicago cards, 1 Atlanta card, and 3 Seattle cards

3. Explain the purpose of the exercise as a team-building activity. Do not indicate that the purpose is to develop *inter*-group teamwork (you want the participants to figure this out).

4. Distribute the "Sleepless in Seattle" Guidelines. Review the rules. Answer all questions requesting clarification of the rules. However, do not reveal the purpose of the exercise.

5. Give each group its envelope. Tell the group they have 30 minutes to complete the activity. If it appears that the groups are not close to completion at the end of 30 minutes, allow some additional time.

6. When the activity is completed, ask the process observers to present their data to their respective groups.

7. After the observers have presented their data, ask the groups to discuss what they might do differently next time if they were to encounter a similar situation.

Debriefing:

Reassemble the total team, and spend some time reviewing the learning points and applications from this game. Facilitate the discussion by using some of the following questions:

- What were some of the significant things that happened in the course of this activity?
- What things were done that helped the process?
- What things hindered effective teaming between the groups?
- When did you figure out the real purpose of the game was to collaborate with the other groups?
- What would you do differently knowing what you know now?
- How is this situation similar to your actual work environment?
- How is it different?
- What are some significant behaviors that you will take away from this activity and perhaps add to a list of ground rules for your team?

Variation:

Don't name the groups by giving them one of the city labels as in step 1. It then becomes the team task to collect all the clue cards *and* guess the name of the activity.

SLEEPLESS IN SEATTLE

GUIDELINES

Purpose: At the end of the 30-minute time period, all the cards containing the clues (facts) about each city should be in the possession of the group designated for that city. For example, all the Seattle clue cards should be in the possession of the "Sleepless in Seattle" group.

Rules:

1. You may give only one card to another group during the course of a single meeting. However, it is not necessary to receive another card in return.

2. Each group should select one person to serve as its negotiator with the other groups. The group may change its negotiator at any time.

3. A negotiations meeting must involve only two groups at any one time. If another group wants to negotiate with one of these two groups, it must wait until the first meeting is over and one negotiator returns to his or her group.

4. The negotiations meetings are the only forums for communications between groups.

Sleepless in Seattle ▼	CNN started here.	The winds are famous here.
Amazon.com was founded here	Mint juleps are great here.	Michael is king here.
Everyone shops at Pike Place here.	**Fearless in Philly** ▼	Some say the blues are the best here.
Seahawks fly here	Rocky trained here.	The Sears Tower is the highest here.
Starbucks started here.	Dr. J. operated here.	Second City Comedy is here.
Salmon is king here.	Eagles soar here.	**Daring in Dallas** ▼
The Space Needle is a beacon here.	The best pretzels are here.	Barbecue is hot here.
Nordstrom's defined customer service here.	A cracked bell is here.	America's team plays here.
Aimless in Atlanta ▼	Billy Penn is a symbol here.	The West End is the place to party here.
Dr. King preached here.	**Clueless in Chicago** ▼	Everything is bigger here.
The Braves win here.	Cubs run free here.	Oil is king here.

SLEEPLESS IN SEATTLE

PROCESS OBSERVER GUIDELINES

Directions: Please sit where you can see and hear most of the team discussions. You are a silent observer—do not speak or in any way participate in the activity. Take notes. Use direct quotes, where possible, that demonstrate a point. Primarily, you are looking for comments or behaviors that helped or hindered the process.

1. **Task Behaviors:** What things helped or hindered the group in its effort to get the job done?

2. **Process Behaviors:** What things helped or hindered the way the group members worked together?

3. **Competitive Behavior:** What types of things did the group do to compete with the other groups?

4. **Collaborative Behavior:** What type of things did the group do to collaborate with the other groups?

5. **Other:** Are there any other things that you noticed that increased or decreased the effectiveness of the team?

A thoughtful way to kick off a team-building session that gets team members to reflect on their image.

SLOGANS
AN INTACT TEAM ICEBREAKER

Purpose:

1. To give team members an opportunity to reflect on the image of the team
2. To provide an opportunity to assess the team with images rather than numbers

Team Size:

Designed for an intact team of less than 10 members; however, it can be adapted for use in a course for team leaders

Required Resources:

A copy of the "Slogans" handout for each person (p. 84)

Time:

30 to 45 minutes

Room Setup:

Chairs in a circle or chairs around a round or rectangular table

Steps:

1. Before the session, determine the outcomes you want to achieve. Do you want to use the exercise primarily as an icebreaker, or do you want it to be more of an assessment activity?
2. Explain the purpose of the activity to the group.
3. Distribute the handout. Ask each person to review the list of slogans and make his or her selection. Alert everyone to the fact that you will ask them to provide the reasons behind their choices.
4. Facilitate a discussion based on the responses. You may begin by going down the list asking if anyone selected each slogan. When you get a positive response, facilitate a discussion on that slogan by asking some of the following questions:

- Why did you select this one?
- What do you think the slogan means (some of the slogans have double meanings)?
- What is it about your team (i.e., what do you all do) that caused you to select this slogan?
- Would you be proud to have this slogan represent you?
- Would you edit or change the slogan in any way to better describe your team?

5. If time permits, discuss the slogans not selected.

Debriefing:

Close the session by reviewing the selected slogans. Ask:

- What does it say about our team that we selected these slogans?
- What does it say about our style? values? strengths? weaknesses?
- Are there other slogans not on the list that you would prefer?
- Does this activity point us in the direction of things that need to change?

Variations:

1. Revise the list of slogans to include others that may be of greater interest to the team.

2. Make a transparency of the handout. Before beginning the discussion (step 4), tally the number of people who selected each slogan. Begin the discussion with the slogan receiving the most votes.

3. Make a game of the tally exercise by asking each person to guess which slogan will receive the most votes. Ask each person to write his or her name and selection on a piece of paper and fold it. Give a small prize to the person who guessed right. In addition, ask that person to begin the discussion by indicating why he or she selected that slogan.

4. Ask the team to rank the slogans. Turn the activity into a consensus-building exercise.

5. If time permits, you can close the activity by having some fun with the slogans. Before the session, delete the names of the companies from the handout. When you close the session, ask the team to name the company associated with each slogan.

This exercise was developed from some material originally prepared by Sapna Shah of Ann Taylor, Inc., New York, NY.

SLOGANS

Directions: Please review the list of slogans and select the one that best represents your team now.

1.	ENDLESS POSSIBILITIES	Liz Claiborne
2.	THE REAL THING	Coca Cola
3.	DRIVERS WANTED	Volkswagen*
4.	THINK DIFFERENT	Apple
5.	OOH LA LA	Sassoon
6.	FIND YOUR OWN ROAD	Saab
7.	PEOPLE MOVING IDEAS	GTE
8.	IN TOUCH WITH TOMORROW	Toshiba
9.	IT'S ALL WITHIN YOUR REACH	AT&T
10.	PEOPLE FINDING A BETTER WAY	Dana
11.	GO FARTHER	Izuzu
12.	WHERE DO YOU WANT TO GO TODAY?	Microsoft

*The full slogan is "On the highway of life there are drivers and passengers. Drivers wanted."

Do you know the stages of team development?

STAGES

REVIEWING THE TEAM-DEVELOPMENT PROCESS

Purpose:

To identify behaviors, attitudes, thoughts, feelings, perceptions, expectations, problems, strategies, and tactics associated with the four stages of team development

Team Size:

9 or more. Organize the participants into three or more groups, each with 3–7 members.

Required Resources:

1. "Stages in Team Development Summary." Reproduce 1 copy for each participant (p. 88)

2. "Item List." Reproduce 1 copy for each participant (p. 89)

3. "Team Record Sheet." Reproduce 1 copy for each group (p. 90)

4. "Correct Classification List." Reproduce 1 copy for the facilitator (p. 91)

Time:

45 minutes

Room Setup:

Chairs around a round or rectangular table for each group

Steps:

1. **Review the stages.** Distribute copies of the "Stages in Team Development" Summary. Guide the participants through the four stages.

2. **Distribute the items to be classified.** Give a copy of the "Item List" to each participant. Explain that these items are related to behaviors, attitudes, thoughts, feelings, perceptions, expectations, problems, strategies, and tactics associated with the four stages of team development. Ask the participants to review the first few items and to identify the stage associated with each.

3. **Demonstrate the task.** Ask the participants to review the first item again and to identify the stage it is associated with. Using the participants' suggestions, show how this item belongs to the *performing* stage.

4. **Team Formation.** Organize the participants into three or more groups of approximately equal numbers. Distribute a copy of the "Team Record Sheet" to each team.

5. **Explain the rules of the game.** You will call out an item number. All groups will review the item, identify the stage of team development it is associated with, and record the appropriate abbreviation on the record sheet. If the item is associated with more than one stage, ask the groups to record all of them.

6. **Explain the scoring system.** You will announce the official answer (based on the opinions of a panel of experts) for the item. Each group that selected the correct stage will receive a point. Each of these groups will also receive an additional point for each team that missed the official answer.

7. **Begin the first round.** Randomly call out an item number. Ask the groups to discuss the item, select the appropriate stage (or stages) in the team-development process, and write down their choice on their "Team Record Sheet."

8. **Monitor the groups.** Circulate among the groups, clarifying the procedure if necessary. Check to see if the groups have recorded their responses. If a group holds up the progress of the game, give it a 10-second time limit to finish.

9. **Announce the official response.** When all the groups have recorded their responses, refer to your Master List and announce the officially determined stage.

10. **Award points.** Award a point for each group that has recorded the correct stage. Then award additional points equal to the number of groups that missed this stage.

11. **Continue the game.** Repeat the same procedure of calling out an item number, asking the groups to record the appropriate stage, announcing the experts' answer, and computing the scores.

12. **Announce an intermission.** At the end of the fifth round, tell the groups to spend the next 3 minutes planning for future rounds. They can use this time to consolidate what they have learned and to review the item list. Pause for 3 minutes and then continue the game as before.

13. **Conclude the game.** At the end of the appropriate time, announce the conclusion of the game. Ask the groups to add up their scores. Identify and congratulate the winning team.

Debriefing:

Ask the participants to discuss what they learned from this game. Use a variety of questions to review the team-development stages and to relate them to the workplace. Here are some suggested questions:

- Which stage is the most difficult one to understand and to apply?
- Which stage should be divided into two (or more) narrower stages? Why?
- Which stages should be combined into a single broader stage? Why?

- Should we add more stages to the process? What additional stages do you suggest? Why?
- Should we remove any stages from the process? Which stages should be removed? Why?
- How does this information help a team increase its effectiveness?
- How would you apply this information to your team or a team that you facilitate?

Variations:

1. Impose a time limit for each round. For example, ask the groups to come up with the correct classification within 60 seconds.

2. If there are differences among group classifications, ask each group to justify its response. Permit groups to change their original classification if necessary.

STAGES IN TEAM DEVELOPMENT

Psychologists who study the behavior of small groups suggest that all teams go through four distinct stages in their development.

1. The first stage in a team's development is *forming*. During this stage, the team members are unsure about what they are doing. Their focus is on understanding the team's goal and their role. They worry about whether the other team members will accept them. Team members frequently look for clarification from their leader.

2. The second stage in a team's development is *storming*. During this stage, the team members try to get their act together. This stage is marked by conflict among the members and between the members and the leader. Through this conflict, the team attempts to define itself.

3. The third stage in a team's development is *norming*. This stage follows storming, after the team members have succeeded in resolving their conflicts. They now feel more secure with one another and with their leader. They effectively negotiate the structure of the team and the division of labor.

4. The fourth stage in a team's development is *performing*. During this stage, the team members behave in a mature fashion and focus on accomplishing their goals. This stage is marked by direct, two-way communication among the team members.

Source: B. W. Tuckman, Developmental sequence in small groups, *Psychological Bulletin, 63*(6), 1965, 384–399.

ITEM LIST

1. All members participate in all team activities.
2. Disagreements become more civilized and less divisive.
3. Feeling of "us-them" increases.
4. Ground rules become second nature to team members.
5. If there is a formal leader, team members tend to obey him or her.
6. Leadership is shared among different members.
7. Leadership role is rotated among appropriate members.
8. Members are anxious and suspicious of the task ahead.
9. Members are more committed to their subgroups than to the team as a whole.
10. Members are more friendly toward one another.
11. Members are not committed to the group's goal.
12. Members are not fully committed to the team goal.
13. Members are proud to be chosen for the team.
14. Members are relieved that things are progressing smoothly.
15. Members are satisfied about the team progress.
16. Members argue with one another, even when they agree on the basic issues.
17. Members attempt to figure out their roles and functions.
18. Members begin to enjoy team activities.
19. Members challenge, evaluate, and destroy ideas.
20. Members choose sides.

TEAM RECORD SHEET

Round	Item Number	Stage	Game Points
1			
2			
3			
4			
5			
6			
7			
8			
9			
10			
11			
12			
13			
14			
15			
16			
17			
18			
19			
20			

CORRECT CLASSIFICATION LIST

Item Number	Stage
1	P
2	N
3	N
4	P
5	F
6	N, P
7	N, P
8	F
9	S
10	N, P
11	F
12	F
13	F
14	N
15	P
16	S
17	N
18	P
19	S
20	S

Here's a fun way to teach the basics of teamwork.

TEAM BINGO

AN EDUCATIONAL ACTIVITY

Purpose:

1. To present some introductory information about teamwork in an interactive fashion
2. To develop some *esprit de corps* among team members

Team Size:

Any number of people can play this game. It is designed to be played in teams of 5 to 8 members.

Required Resources:

1. A copy of the "Team Bingo" card for each person (p. 94)
2. A list of the "Team Bingo Questions and Answers" for the facilitator (p. 95)

Time:

30 minutes

Room Setup:

Clusters of tables and chairs set around the room for each team

Steps:

1. Explain the purpose of the activity by emphasizing that it will be a fun alternative to a lecture about teamwork concepts and terms. If necessary, before the session ask everyone to read a handout or excerpt from a book that contains information about teamwork concepts and terms. One good source is Peter Scholtes and others, *The Team Handbook* (Madison, WI: Joiner Associates, 1988).
2. Distribute the Team Bingo card to everyone. Review the rules.
3. Begin reading the items from the Team Bingo Questions.
4. Keep reading the questions until all the items have been covered.

Debriefing:

Conclude the session by asking if anyone would like more information about any of the items.

- Ask what new teamwork terms participants learned from the activity.
- Ask how participants would change the game to increase what is learned.

Variations:

1. Consider giving small prizes to the winning team or all teams that get bingo before all questions are read. Prizes need to be something that can be shared by all team members, such as a bag of candy.
2. Edit the items to include some of your company- or team-specific items.

TEAM BINGO

self-directed work team	group incentive	project team reward	role clarification	consensus
norms	sponsor	facilitator	parking lot	virtual team
listening	coaching	cross-functional team	quality circles	storming
project team	Pareto principle	85/15 rule	flow chart	Pareto chart
cause-and-effect diagram	multivoting	nominal group technique	100-mile rule	gate keeper

TEAM BINGO
QUESTIONS AND ANSWERS

Directions: The first person to jump up or raise his or her hand will be allowed to answer the question. If the answer is correct, his or her team will be able to put an "X" through the box containing that answer. If the answer is incorrect, the team will be required to eliminate an "X" already on their card or, if they have no Xs, they will not participate in the next round. If the answer is incorrect, the second team will be given an opportunity to answer the question, if they so choose, with the same potential penalty.

The first team to get five Xs in a row—vertical, horizontal, or diagonal—will be the winner.

1. A group of people with a common goal who work in different locations and may never (or only rarely) meet face-to-face. (Answer: **virtual team**)
2. A skill often required of supervisors and managers who support teams in their organization. (Answer: **coaching**)
3. A team concept, popularized by Japanese companies, that brings together workers to solve problems and improve work processes. (Answer: **quality circles**)
4. An ad hoc group that comes together for a defined period of time to solve a problem or accomplish a goal. (Answer: **project team**)
5. The rule of thumb that says that a large majority of an organization's problems can be corrected only by changing systems and that a very small percentage of problems are under the worker's control. (Answer: **85/15**)
6. A series of bars whose heights reflect the frequency of impact of problems. (Answer: **Pareto chart**)
7. A method similar to a straw poll used to reduce a long list of items to a short list of the most important or popular items. (Answer: **multivoting**)
8. A team norm that is used to prevent members from being called out of a meeting unnecessarily. (Answer: **100-mile rule**)
9. A bonus given to all members of a division, plant, or other large organizational unit. (Answer: **group incentive**)
10. A technique used to share and gain agreement on a set of expectations for each team member. (Answer: **role clarification**)
11. The rules of the road or set of behavioral guidelines that are developed by and agreed to by all team members. (Answer: **norms**)
12. The person responsible for managing the process aspects of a team meeting. (Answer: **facilitator**)
13. The individual skill most needed and most often lacking in team members. (Answer: **listening**)
14. A team composed of people from different parts of the organization. (Answer: **cross-functional team**)
15. The stage in team development characterized by conflict among team members. (Answer: **storming**)
16. The rule of thumb that says that 80% of the trouble comes from 20% of the problems. (Answer: **Pareto principle**)
17. A step-by-step schematic that describes a process that is to be studied. (Answer: **flow chart**)
18. Known as a "fishbone," this tool allows a team to map out the factors thought to affect a problem. (Answer: **cause-and-effect diagram**)
19. A structured approach to generating a list of options that is characterized by a minimal amount of interaction among team members. (Answer: **nominal group technique**)
20. The person responsible for encouraging a more or less equal amount of participation among team members by involving quiet people and reducing domination by others. (Answer: **gate keeper**)
21. A team of people responsible for a process, product, or service or a significant part thereof with little or minimal supervision. (Answer: **self-directed work team**)
22. A bonus awarded to a team for the accomplishment of a specific goal. (Answer: **project team reward**)
23. A decision-making process that results in an outcome that is acceptable enough that everyone can support it and no member opposes it. (Answer: **consensus**)
24. A manager who helps a team reach its goals by providing support and resources and eliminating barriers. (Answer: **sponsor**)
25. Usually a sheet of flip-chart paper on which team members write items to be addressed at some future time. (Answer: **parking lot**)

Put your money where your team's idea is!

TEAM CONTEST
AN IDEA-GENERATION CHALLENGE

Purpose:

1. To generate creative ideas for increasing and improving teamwork in your organization

2. To persuade people to accept the team's ideas by writing clear and compelling descriptions

Team Size:

10 to 30 participants, divided into teams of 3 to 7 members each

Required Resources:

1. Blank sheets of paper
2. $10 as seed money for prizes
3. Access to a photocopying machine
4. Timer
5. Whistle

Time:

90 minutes

Room Setup:

Chairs around tables for each team

Steps:

1. **Organize teams.** Divide the players into teams of three or more members. It does not matter if some teams have an extra member.

2. **Explain the team task.** Each team is invited to submit one or more creative ideas that will increase and improve teamwork in an organization. The idea, which may

focus on removing obstacles or utilizing opportunities or a combination of both approaches, should be submitted on a single page. Each idea should have a short title. There will be an entrance fee of $5 per idea. A team may submit any number of ideas (at the cost of $5 per idea).

3. **Announce the prizes.** You will contribute $10 to the prize-money pool. All entrance fees will be added to this amount. The ideas submitted by different teams will be evaluated and ranked. The top three ideas will divide the prize money in the ratio of 5:3:2.

   For example, if six ideas were submitted, the total prize money will be $10 + (6 \times $5) = $40. The first prize will be $20, the second prize $12, and the third prize $8.

4. **Start the teamwork session.** Announce a suitable time limit. Ask the teams to use their creative thinking skills and come up with one or more ideas. Emphasize that they should generate effective ideas and write them up in a clear and compelling fashion.

5. **Conclude the activity.** At the end of the time limit, blow the whistle and ask the teams to stop whatever they are doing. Ask each team to submit its idea (or ideas) along with the entrance fee(s).

6. **Make copies of the ideas.** Send your helper to photocopy a complete set of the ideas for each team. While the idea sheets are being copied, conduct a mini-debriefing or let the participants take a break.

7. **Ask the teams to evaluate ideas.** Give each team a complete set of ideas. Ask the team to award 1 to 9 points for each idea, except its own. Announce a suitable time limit.

8. **Prepare a score board.** List the titles of all ideas on a flip chart.

9. **Consolidate the scores.** Blow the whistle and ask the teams to complete their evaluation activity. Read off each title from the flip chart and ask different teams for the number of points they awarded to that idea. Add these points and write the total in the appropriate space.

10. **Award the prizes.** Find the ideas that received the top three total scores. Divide the prize money into 10 equal parts. Award five parts to the team with the highest score, three parts to the team with the second-highest score, and two parts to the team with the third-highest score. (If two teams are tied for the highest score, combine the prize money for the first two places and split it equally between the two teams. If three or more teams are tied with the highest score, divide the prize money equally among the teams.)

Debriefing:

While waiting for the photocopies to be made, conduct a discussion of participants' experiences. Here are some suggested questions:

- How did you make decisions in your team?
- How did you work on generating ideas?

- How did you write up your ideas?
- Did different team members take charge of different tasks, or did the same members work on all tasks?
- How would you organize your team and structure your activity if we were to conduct the contest all over again?
- How is the way you worked on this task different from (or similar to) the way your team works back in the workplace?

At the end of the activity, ask participants to discuss these types of questions:

- What criteria did you use for evaluating different ideas?
- How did you distribute the evaluation task among different team members?
- Did the scores awarded to your team's idea surprise you? If so, in what way?
- What did you learn about team development, trust, and decision making?

Varations:

1. To speed up the game, ask teams to write their ideas on flip-chart paper, and tape it to the wall. To determine the winning teams, give colored dots to the teams and ask them to place these dots among the different ideas (except their own).

2. To slow down the game, play it in installments: During the first meeting, organize the teams and explain the contest rules. Announce a suitable due date. Let the teams work on their own and submit their entry forms (and entrance fees) to you. Some time after the due date, conduct another meeting, distribute copies of the idea sheets, ask teams to evaluate them, consolidate the scores, and award cash prizes to the winning teams.

3. To make the evaluation more objective, give a rating scale to each team for evaluating the ideas. Ask an external judge or a panel of experts to review the entries and select the winners. You can also use a few selected participants as a panel of judges. During the activity, these participants can be process observers providing data during the first debriefing period.

Making decisions about making decisions.

TEAM DECISIONS
STRUCTURED BRAINSTORMING

Purpose:

1. To generate suitable guidelines for decision making in teams

2. To arrange these guidelines in order of usefulness

Team Size:

9 to 30 participants arranged into 3 to 6 teams of 3 to 7 participants

Required Resources:

1. Paper and pencil

2. Flip chart and markers

3. Timer

4. Whistle

Time:

45 minutes

Room Setup:

Chairs around a round table for each team

Steps:

1. **Set the context.** Explain that the game deals with decision making in teams. Ask the participants to give recent examples of decisions made by their teams. Post the responses on a flip chart.

2. **Form teams.** Divide the participants into an appropriate number of teams. Ask each team to brainstorm five guidelines for effective decision making. Suggest that each team should brainstorm several items, select the five best guidelines, and record them on a piece of paper.

3. **Create a common list.** Ask each team to take turns calling out one of the best guidelines from its list. Paraphrase these guidelines on a flip chart. During later rounds, ask the teams to make sure that their new guideline is different from those already listed. Continue this procedure until the common list contains 10 guidelines.

4. **Select the top guidelines.** Ask each team to review the guidelines on the common list, select the guideline that appears to be the most powerful, and write its number on a small piece of paper. Collect these pieces of paper and read them. Explain that since your goal is to reward consensus, you will award each team a score that equals the number of teams selecting the same guideline.

5. **Rank and eliminate the top guideline.** Draw a line through the guideline that was selected by the most teams. Indicate its top rank by putting an "I" in the front of the guideline.

6. **Continue the play of the game.** Ask the teams to select the next most powerful guideline from the list. Repeat this process of selection, scoring, and elimination. If no clear-cut item emerges as the most powerful guideline at the end of a round, do not eliminate any item. Instead, declare a 2-minute debate period during which each team attempts to persuade the other teams to vote with them.

7. **Conclude the game.** Repeat the procedure until the teams have identified the top five guidelines. At this time, announce the end of the game.

8. **Identify the winning team.** The team with the highest total score wins the Recognition Award for being the best identifier of powerful guidelines. There is another category for winning the game, based on the teams' original lists. Teams identify guidelines that made the top five. Each team scores 5 points for having included the first-ranked guideline, 4 points for the next, and so on. The team with the highest total of these points wins the Originality Award. Give each winning team a prize that can be divided among the members (for example, bag of candies).

Debriefing:

Ask each team to create a rating scale incorporating the top five decision-making guidelines. Post the scale on the flip chart. Then ask members of each team to apply the rating scale to evaluate its own behavior in making decisions during the game.

Variations:

1. If you have fewer than six players, conduct the game as an individual-player activity.

2. Conclude the game after identifying the top five guidelines. Skip the step of identifying winning teams.

3. Begin with a prepared set of 10 guidelines for decision making in teams. Ask the teams to select the top-rated guideline.

Here's a fun game that everyone knows and loves.

TEAM GAME SHOW

A COMPETITIVE ACTIVITY

Purpose:

1. To provide participants with a positive, competitive activity
2. To provide a review of some teamwork concepts
3. To open or close a team event with a high-energy activity

Team Size:

Works best with a group of 25 to 35 participants divided into teams of 5 to 7. We have played the game with as many as 60 people. If the group is smaller, reduce the number of teams. Each team should have a minimum of 4 members.

Required Resources:

1. A copy of the "Team Game Show Categories" for the facilitator (p. 103)
2. A copy of the "Team Game Show Guidelines" for each player (p. 105)
3. A transparency copy of the "Team Game Show Board" (p. 106)
4. Overhead projector, screen, and projector pen
5. Flip chart, pad, and markers

Time:

30 to 45 minutes

Room Setup:

Chairs around a round or rectangular table for each team, set in a semicircle around the room. Table with overhead projector and the flip chart stand at the head of the room.

Steps:

1. Explain the purpose of the activity. Form teams and have them sit together at separate tables. Ask for a volunteer to serve as scribe. Ask the scribe to create a score sheet with a column for each team on the flip chart.

2. Review the "Team Game Guidelines" at the same time that the "Team Game Show Board" is displayed on the overhead projector. Take questions to clarify the rules.

3. Give each team 2 minutes to plan their strategy.

4. Select the first category and point combination. The scribe records the points scored on the flip chart and crosses off the category/point box on the Game Board overhead.

5. Continue the game until all questions have been answered. The scribe tallies the team scores.

6. Ask the teams to get ready for the final round by deciding how many points they want to wager. Allow 20 seconds for this decision.

7. The final round question should be a tough question about a team or teams in your organization. If you cannot come up with a question, you can use one of the following:

   - He is the primary author of the all-time, best-selling book about teams, *The Team Handbook*. Who is Peter Scholtes?

   - The person who watches for specific behaviors during meetings, takes notes, and later reports his or her findings. What is a process observer?

   - The single most important factor that distinguishes high-performing teams from all other teams. What is a clear goal (performance objective)?

8. Tally the final score and declare the winner. Ask if any of the questions or answers were confusing or require a bit more explanation. Give out prizes to the winning team.

Debriefing:

Ask the teams to meet and discuss the activity in terms of what they learned about teamwork, process, and competition.

   - Facilitate a general discussion of the views of each of the teams. Post the learning points on the flip chart.

Variations:

1. Change the categories and/or questions to be more closely aligned with your team or organization. Other categories you might use include competitors, market trends, company products/services, company locations/divisions, and team results (e.g., cost savings, new ideas, new products).

2. If time permits (or as a pre-work assignment), ask teams to come up with questions for a particular category.

Adapted from materials originally prepared by Sapna Shah and Andra Ehrenkrnaz of Ann Taylor, Inc., New York, NY.

TEAM GAME SHOW CATEGORIES

Television Show Teams

Points	Question	Answer
100	A team of two female New York City cops known by their last names	*Cagney & Lacey*
200	A team of three glamorous female private detectives who communicate with their boss only via phone	*Charlie's Angels*
300	A show about a lovable team of varied characters who spend most of their time hanging out at a neighborhood bar	*Cheers*
400	A blended family team	*Brady Bunch*
500	A show about a team of high tech specialists headed by a leader known only as Mr. Phelps	*Mission Impossible*

Types of Teams

Points	Question	Answer
100	An ad hoc team of people who come together to solve a problem or achieve a goal and then disband	project team
200	A team of people who all work in different departments or disciplines	cross-functional team
300	A team of people who work together but never or only rarely have a face-to-face meeting	virtual team
400	A cross-functional group designed to come up with ways of improving internal operations or processes	redesign, or systems reengineering
500	A team of people who work together every day in the same office, location, machine, or process	natural work group

Business Teams

Points	Question	Answer
100	The car company where everyone is a member of a team	Saturn
200	A book about the team that built a new computer at Data General	Soul of a New Machine
300	The name of the computer where everyone on the design team signed his/her name on the back of it	Macintosh
400	The name of the company that includes the word "Team" as part of their company name	Xerox
500	Named for an animal, this is a team that operates outside of the normal business organization	Skunk Works

Sports Teams

100	The basketball team that won four world champions in the 1990s	Chicago Bulls
200	The baseball stadium that is known as "the house that Ruth built"	Yankee Stadium
300	The country that Pelé, the soccer super star, played for	Brazil
400	The college that the "four horsemen and seven blocks of granite" played for	Notre Dame
500	The championship hockey team that was known as the "Broad Street Bullies"	Philadelphia Flyers

Famous Teams

100	The historical site that honors a team of four famous U.S. presidents	Mt. Rushmore
200	The musical group from Liverpool that took the world by storm during the early 1960s	Beatles
300	The best known team of U.S. astronauts	Apollo 11
400	The song-writing team that created the music for such Broadway hits as "South Pacific"	Rogers & Hammerstein
500	The team of scientists who secretly created the atomic bomb during the second world war	Manhattan Project

Team Process Concepts

100	A tool that results in a decision that all team members can "live with"	consensus
200	The team member who tries to equalize participation by encouraging quiet people to speak out and reducing the impact of monopolizers	gate keeper
300	The communciation skill that is most needed by teams	active listening
400	The behavioral expectations or rules that guide and shape team member participation	norms
500	A step-by-step schematic picture used to plan the stages of a project or describe a work process	flow chart

TEAM GAME GUIDELINES

Players:

- Must phrase their response in the form of a question
- Must be the first one to stand up in order to answer the question
- Must abide by the decision of the facilitator as to who stood up first
- May use any workshop materials as reference tools for any question
- May, if they wish, wager all of their points on the final round

Rules:

- The first category/point combination will be chosen by the facilitator.
- Then, the team that correctly answered the previous question chooses the next category and point combination.
- In the final round, each team confers for 20 seconds to decide how many points they want to wager. All teams are eligible to play the final round.
- 1-minute time limit for any question

Logistics:

- Facilitator will lead the game and read the questions.
- Facilitator will have the correct answers.
- Scribe will keep track of which questions have been answered. He/She will mark off questions answered on the overhead transparency.
- Scribe will also keep the team scores on the flip chart.
- The team that wins will receive prizes for every team member.

TEAM GAME SHOW BOARD

TV TEAMS	TYPES OF TEAMS	BUSINESS TEAMS	SPORTS TEAMS	FAMOUS TEAMS	TEAM PROCESS CONCEPTS
100	100	100	100	100	100
200	200	200	200	200	200
300	300	300	300	300	300
400	400	400	400	400	400
500	500	500	500	500	500

Have your camera ready—this activity provides a great photo op.

TEAM HATS
A CLOSING ACTIVITY

Purpose:

1. To close a team-building session on a positive note
2. To provide members of an intact team with positive, playful feedback

Team Size:

Works best with an intact team of less than 10. However, it can be used with a large group or training class that has been working together in a series of teams for at least 1 day.

Required Resources:

1. A white painter's hat or similar white cotton hat for each person. In addition to finding hats at your local paint, hardware, or home center store, the hats are available from The Trainers' Warehouse, 89-1 Washington Avenue, Natick, MA 01760, 1-800-299-3770.
2. Lots of felt-tip markers in a variety of colors
3. A bag or box

Time:

30 minutes

Room Setup:

Chairs around a round or rectangular table

Steps:

1. Before the session, write the name of each person on a small piece of paper. Fold the paper so that the name cannot be seen. Put the pieces of paper in a bag or box
2. Place a large number of different-colored markers in the center of the table.
3. Distribute a hat to each person.

4. Pass the bag or box around and ask each person to select a piece of paper. If a person selects his or her own name, he or she should return it and pick another piece of paper.

5. Explain that each person should decorate the hat with words, drawings, sayings, and/or logos that he or she feels represent the person selected. Emphasize that the decorations should be positive. The person's name should also be clearly printed on the hat.

6. When everyone is finished, the hats should be exchanged so that each person has the hat that has been prepared for him or her.

7. Ask each person to show his or her hat to the group and describe his or her reactions to it.

   • How does he/she feel about the decorations?

   • Does he/she understand all the decorations?

   • Does he/she agree with them?

   • What other items would he/she have added to this hat?

   • How does he/she feel about wearing the hat now?

   • Would he/she wear the hat outside the session?

8. At some point take a picture of the team with everyone wearing their hats. After the session, get a sufficient number of reprints so that each person gets a copy of the picture.

Debriefing:

Conclude the session with a brief discussion of the value of the activity.

   • How do you feel about the activity?

   • How did it help us grow as a team?

   • What should we do with the hats?

   • Should we wear the hats at our next team meeting?

Variations:

1. Use name card tents instead of hats.

2. Ask each person to decorate his or her own hat.

Do you have what it takes to be a team leader?

TEAM LEADER

IDENTIFYING DESIRABLE CHARACTERISTICS OF LEADERS

Purpose:

1. To identify the desirable characteristics of effective team leaders
2. To evaluate the behaviors of a team leader

Team Size:

Best for 15 to 30 participants, divided into teams of 3 to 7 members

Required Resources:

1. Copies of handout 1, "Team Leader Talent Search" (p. 112), for each participant
2. Copies of handout 2, "Characteristics of Effective Team Leaders" (p. 113), for each participant
3. Flip chart
4. Felt markers
5. Timer
6. Whistle

Time:

45 minutes

Room Setup:

Chairs around rectangular or round tables for each team

Steps:

1. **Advertise yourself.** Distribute copies of handout 1, "Team Leader Talent Search." Ask the participants to read the handout and write an ad to sell their services as a team leader. Announce a 3-minute time limit for this activity.

2. **Form teams.** Divide the participants into 3–5 teams of 3–7 members each. The teams should be of approximately equal size (some teams may have an extra member). Ask the members of each team to sit near one another and away from the other teams.

3. **Collect and distribute the ads.** Collect the ads from each team, making sure that they all have an ID number. Keep the ads from each team as a separate packet. Give the set of ads from one team to the next team.

4. **Review the ads and select a team leader.** Ask each team to review the ads and select a candidate for team-leader job. The team should involve all its members in this selection process, and it may use any criteria for choosing the team leader. Announce a 5-minute time limit for this activity.

5. **Assign team leaders to teams.** Ask each team to read the ID number of the selected candidate. Identify and assign each selected team leader to the team that selected him or her. (In this process, each team will lose a member and gain a team leader.)

6. **Identify desirable characteristics of team leaders.** Ask the team leaders to lead their teams through the next activity. Each team should make a list of desirable characteristics of team leaders. Team members may review the ads to identify desirable characteristics reflected in them. The team has 5 minutes to identify 5 or more desirable characteristics of team leaders.

7. **Compare with the master list.** Ask each team to read its list of desirable characteristics of team leaders. Record these items on a flip chart. Distribute copies of handout 2, "Characteristics of Effective Team Leaders." Explain that this list is based on a review of the literature on team leadership. Ask each team leader to conduct a discussion in his or her team to compare the team's list with the master list. Announce a 5-minute time limit for this activity.

8. **Compare words with actions.** As a final activity, ask each team to read the ad written by its team leader. Ask the team members to discuss whether the team leader's behaviors equaled, exceeded, or fell short of the promises made in the ad. Assign a 3-minute time limit for this activity. Instruct the team leaders to silently receive this feedback.

Debriefing:

Conduct a discussion of the insights gained by different participants. Here are some suggested questions:

- What factors did you emphasize in writing your ad?
- What factors did you use in reviewing different ads?
- How did you feel about not being selected as a team leader? For those who were chosen, how did you feel about being selected as a team leader?
- Each team conducted its first activity (of selecting the best team-leader candidate) without a team leader and the next activity (of listing desirable characteristics of team leaders) with a team leader. Was there a difference in the performance of the team?

- What is the most important insight you got from this activity?
- Was there a difference between what the team leader promised in the ad and how he or she behaved? If so, what do you think were the reasons for the difference?
- If each selected team leader won a $50 cash award, how would your behaviors and reactions have changed?
- If you were a team leader, how did you react to the final activity when the team members discussed your behavior? Was it difficult for you to listen to the feedback without feeling defensive?

TEAM LEADER TALENT SEARCH

As you know, our organization is vigorously implementing its rapid workteam deployment policy. We are also committed to hiring talented team leaders within the organization.

We are conducting a talent search for hiring a new group of team leaders. We want every employee to take part in this talent search. Please write an ad of 75 words listing the reason why you believe that you would make an effective team leader. Please do not use artwork or graphics of any kind. Write your ad in the space below to attract potential teams to hire you. Be sure to flaunt all your unique competencies and desirable qualities.

Since the selection committee wants to choose the leader exclusively on the basis of his or her talents and characteristics, please do not include your name in your ad. Instead, use an ID number. Choose any four-digit number that you can easily recall later.

Your ID number: _____

_____

_____

_____

_____

_____

_____

_____

_____

_____

_____

_____

_____

_____

CHARACTERISTICS OF EFFECTIVE TEAM LEADERS

- Coaching skills
- Confidence
- Consistency between word and deed
- Creativity
- Empathic listening skills
- Having a vision
- Inspiring
- Integrity
- Long-term focus
- Maintaining a balance between individual needs and team needs
- Realism
- Self-esteem
- Sense of priorities
- Service mentality
- Sincerity
- Technical expertise
- Trust
- Willingness to share responsibility
- Willingness to share credits

You know each norm, but how do the norms work together?

TEAM NORMS

EXPLORING RELATIONSHIPS AMONG GROUND RULES

Purpose:

1. To explore the relationship among different norms
2. To reduce inconsistencies among different norms

Time:

30 to 45 minutes

Team Size:

10 or more participants, organized into 5 teams

Required Resources:

1. Individual copies of a 5 × 5 square grid. Both the columns and rows are numbered as in the handout (p. 117). Each square in the grid is marked with its column and row numbers. The squares in the diagonal that have the same row and column numbers are outlined with thicker lines. The squares above this diagonal have a plus (+) sign; the squares below, a minus (-) sign.
2. A large version of this grid on a sheet of flip-chart paper taped to the wall
3. Post-it Notes™
4. Sticky-backed colored dots

Steps:

1. **Form teams.** Organize the participants into five teams of approximately equal size. Ask members of each team to sit together around a table. Distribute individual copies of the grid to each participant.
2. **Brief the participants.** Write the following five norms on a flip chart, each norm with its number in front.
   ① Do your homework.
   ② Ask questions.

③ Be honest.

④ Respect your teammates.

⑤ Satisfy your customers.

Discuss the norms by asking the participants to give their own definitions and examples.

3. **Explain the grid.** Point out that the row and column numbers refer to each of the team norms. The pair of numbers in each square of the grid refers to the relationship between the two norms. For example, the square labeled 34 refers to the relationship between Norm 3 and Norm 4 in the list. Point out that the squares on one of the diagonals has a pair of identical numbers. In this case, the numbers refer to the critical feature of the corresponding norm.

4. **Specify the statements.** Explain that the teams will be required to write statements associated with different squares on the grid, relating the column norm with the row norm.

- The statements for the squares with the same row and column norms on the diagonal should highlight the most critical feature of the norm. For example, the square labeled 44 refers to the critical feature of norm 4.

  SAMPLE: For square 11: Doing your homework involves being accountable for the task delegated to you and for the promises you made.

- The statements for the squares with a plus sign (above the diagonal) should emphasize a positive connection between the two norms. Each statement should indicate how the two norms support and strengthen each other.

  SAMPLE: For square 23 (+): Honest people are not reluctant to ask questions because they have no need to cover up their ignorance.

- The statements for the squares with a minus sign (below the diagonal) should emphasize a negative connection. Each statement should indicate how the two norms clash or interfere with each other.

  SAMPLE: For square 54 (-): Sometimes your customer may have a legitimate complaint about your teammate. In this case, your agreeing with the customer may suggest a lack of respect to your teammate.

5. **Assign columns.** Assign two columns from the grid to each team in this way:

   Team A: Columns 1 and 2.
   Team B: Columns 2 and 3.
   Team C: Columns 3 and 4.
   Team D: Columns 4 and 5.
   Team E: Columns 5 and 1.

   This ensures that each team has two columns and each column is assigned to two different teams.

6. **Ask teams to write statements.** Distribute Post-it Notes™ to each team and ask team members to write a suitable statement for each of the squares in the columns assigned to it. Assign a 10-minute time limit. Encourage the teams to generate alternative statements for each square and to select the best one for the Note.

7. **Conclude the statement-writing activity.** Start a timer and, after 9 minutes, give a 1-minute warning. At the end of the time period, ask participants to stop writing statements and to stick their statements to the appropriate squares in the grid on the wall. You should end up with two statements in each square.

8. **Ask participants to evaluate the statements.** Give a supply of sticky colored dots to participants. Ask each participant to review the squares that do not contain a statement written by his or her team and to stick a colored dot to indicate the better one of the two statements in each square. Assign a suitable time limit for this activity.

9. **Determine the winning team.** After the evaluation task is completed, ask each team to count the number of colored dots stuck to the statements written by it. Identify the team with the most colored dots and declare it to be the winning team. Provide an appropriate prize to the winning team.

Debriefing:

Review the purpose for conducting the activity: to look at the team norms as an interrelated collection rather than as individual items. Ask the participants for insights gained from the activity. Discuss strategies for reducing inconsistencies and conflicts among different norms and for strengthening positive linkages.

Variations:

Ask the team to generate its own set of norms. Select the top five norms and use them in this activity.

15 (+)	25 (+)	25 (+)	45 (+)	55
14 (+)	24 (+)	34 (+)	44	54 (−)
13 (+)	23 (+)	33	43 (−)	53 (−)
12 (+)	22	32 (−)	42 (−)	52 (−)
11	21 (−)	31 (−)	41 (−)	51 (−)

An icebreaker that introduces both the participants and the subject of teamwork.

TEAM QUOTES
AN INTRODUCTORY ACTIVITY

Purpose:

1. To introduce the participants in a team-training class
2. To introduce the subject of teamwork
3. To have participants share some of their feelings about teams and teamwork

Time Size:

Works best with a group of less than 15 people; however, if the group is larger, the activity can be done in several sub-groups

Required Resources:

1. A set of the quote cards (p. 120). It is helpful to have more cards than there are participants. Copy page 120 onto card stock and cut each quote into an individual card.
2. Flip chart, pad, markers, masking tape or push pins

Time:

30 to 45 minutes depending on the size of the group

Room Setup:

Chairs set around a rectangular or round table

Steps:

1. Explain the purpose of the activity.
2. Shuffle the deck of cards. Distribute 1 card to each person.
3. Ask each person to read the card and think about its implications for teamwork, then explain that each person will be asked to introduce him- or herself to the group by indicating the following:
   - Name

- Job
- Location
- Length of time with the organization
- His or her quote and at least one of the following things about the quote:
  —why it's important for successful teamwork
  —how it makes a person a better team player
  —how they personally do these things

Allow 3 minutes for people to prepare their introductions.

Debriefing:

After everyone has introduced him- or herself, ask the group to note key points about teams and teamwork that came out of these introductions. Post the responses on the flip chart.

- Comment on the responses and, as appropriate, indicate how they will be addressed during the remainder of the class.
- Close the activity by asking how it helped team development or the learning process and how participants will be able to use the information in the future.

Variations:

1. If time permits, show the unused cards one at a time and ask for comments from the class similar to those outlined in step 3.

2. Change the directions in step 3: ask each person to describe a personal experience— positive or negative—from his or her past work on teams that is reflective of the quote.

3. For additional quotes, see the activity, "Words to Team By."

The quotes used in this exercise come from two fun little books by Doug McCallum, *The Speed of the Leader . . . Determines the Rate of the Pack* (1996) and *Don't Send Your Turkeys to Eagle School* (1994) published by Tool Thyme For Trainers, 4108 Grace King Place, Metairie, LA 70002, 504-887-5558.

Nothing great was ever achieved without enthusiasm.	The future belongs to those who believe in the beauty of their dreams. *Eleanor Roosevelt*	Even if you are on the right track, you'll get run over if you just sit there. *Will Rogers*
Yesterday ended last night.	People will forget how fast you did a job—but they will always remember how well you did it. *Howard W. Newton*	A great pleasure in life is doing what people say you cannot do. *Walter Gagehot*
In great attempts, it is glorious even to fail.	Nothing of importance was ever done without a plan.	Success is getting up one more time than you fall.
Nothing ruins the truth like stretching it.	One cannot climb a ladder by pushing others down.	Many of life's failures are men and women who did not realize how close they were to success when they gave up.
If the going gets easy, you may be going downhill.	Careful listening helps us see things more clearly.	You always have time for things you put first.

Here's a real-time decision-making exercise that will have some practical pay-off.

TEAM REWARDS

A CONSENSUS ACTIVITY

Purpose:

1. To practice reaching a team-based consensus
2. To share and explore types of rewards that are valued by team members
3. To reach agreement on appropriate forms of rewards for your team

Team Size:

Designed for an intact team of 10 or less; however, can be used in a large group meeting where a variety of teams are seated together

Required Resources:

1. A copy of "Team Rewards: A Consensus Activity" for each person (p. 123)
2. A copy of the Team Process Review for each person (re-use p. 30)
3. Flip chart, pad, markers, masking tape or push pins

Time:

2 hours

Room Setup:

Chairs set around a rectangular or round table

Steps:

1. Explain the purpose of the activity.
2. Distribute copies of the handout "Team Rewards." Ask each person to privately complete the individual ranking of the items in the left column. Allow 5 to 7 minutes.
3. Ask the team to reach a consensus on the ranking of the 10 items. Allow 30 minutes.
4. Ask team members to complete the "Team Process Review" handout.

Debriefing:

- Facilitate a discussion of the team's decision-making process based on the hand-out. Post key learning points on the flip chart.

- Close the session by exploring subsequent steps in terms of implementing the highest-ranked rewards.

Variation:

1. If time is short, ask team members to fill out their individual ranking before the session.

2. Eliminate the team consensus-ranking activity. Facilitate a discussion that focuses on the rewards that allows team members to share their values and learn what others believe about team rewards.

TEAM REWARDS:
A CONSENSUS ACTIVITY

Directions: Please review the list of rewards and rank them in order of greatest positive impact on the team. Place a "1" next to the item that you believe will have the most positive impact on the team and so on down to a "10" next to the item that will have the least impact on the team.

Step 1: Rank the items privately and place your individual ranking in the left column.

Step 2: Arrive at a team consensus on the ranking of the items and place those numbers in the right column.

Individual	Team Reward	Team
	Take a course together	
	Give each team member a $200 check	
	Each member may select a $200 gift from a catalogue	
	Give money ($200 × number of team members) to the local chapter of the Special Olympics	
	Have a team dinner with spouses and significant others	
	Buy a piece of equipment, software, or other big job aid to be used by the whole team	
	Buy a team jacket for each person	
	Have a team party and invite your customers	
	Give membership in a professional organization to each team member	
	Have a team dinner with the president of the company or some other senior executive	

May we have the envelopes, please!

TEAM VALUES
CLARIFYING APPLICATION OPPORTUNITIES

Purpose:

1. To explore everyday applications of five important team values
2. To consolidate brainstormed ideas

Team Size:

8 to 30 participants divided into 4 to 5 teams of fewer than 7 members

Required Resources:

1. Five *Team Value* envelopes. Write one of these values on the front of each envelope: *quality, commitment to the team's vision, integrity, belief in fellow team members,* and *diversity.*
2. Response cards—a packet of index cards for each team
3. Timer
4. Whistle

Time:

45 minutes

Room Setup:

Chairs around a table for each team; tables arranged in a roughly circular format

Steps:

1. **Organize the participants.** Divide the participants into three or more teams of fewer than seven members. Teams should be approximately the same size. Seat the teams in a circular configuration to facilitate the exchange of envelopes.

124

2. **Brief the participants.** Review the five team values one at a time. Explain to the participants that the activity requires them to translate these values into everyday on-the-job decisions and behaviors.

3. **Distribute the supplies.** Give one value envelope to each team. Also give each team four index cards.

4. **Conduct the first round.** Ask team members to discuss the team value written on the envelope they received, and to identify how this value can be incorporated into everyday on-the-job behaviors and decisions. Tell them to write these examples in short sentences on one of the index cards. Encourage teams to write as many sentences as possible, all on the same index card. Announce a time limit of 3 minutes for this activity, and encourage the teams to work rapidly. Explain that the teams' response cards will be eventually evaluated in terms of both the number and the quality of the items.

5. **Conclude the first round.** After 3 minutes, blow the whistle to announce the end of the first round. Explain that each team should place its response card (the index card with its application examples) inside the envelope and pass the envelope, unsealed, to the next team. Ask the teams not to open the envelope they receive.

6. **Conduct the second round.** Ask the teams to review the team value on the envelope they received, but *not* to look at the application examples on the response card inside. Tell the teams to repeat the first-round procedure and to list the everyday applications of this value on a new response card. After 3 minutes, blow the whistle and ask the teams to place the response card inside the envelope and pass it to the next team.

7. **Conduct more rounds.** Conduct two more rounds of the game, using the same procedure.

8. **Conduct the evaluation round.** Start this round just as you did the previous rounds. However, explain to the teams that they do not have to write any more application examples. Instead, the teams must evaluate the four response cards inside the envelope. They do this by reviewing the individual examples on each response card and then comparing the cards with one another on the basis of their overall effect. The teams have 100 points to distribute among the four response cards to indicate each card's relative merits. Announce a suitable time limit for this evaluation activity.

9. **Present the results.** At the end of the time limit, check on the teams to ensure they have completed their task and have recorded score points on each response card. Select a team at random to present its evaluation results. Ask the team to announce the team value written on the envelope it received and to read the application examples on each card, beginning with the card that received the least number of points. The team should progress from one card to the next in an ascending order of the number of points. After reading all four cards, the team should announce how it distributed the 100 points and briefly explain the criteria used for distributing the points.

10. **Determine the winner.** Instruct the teams to place all the response cards on a table at the front of the room; then call for a representative from each team to collect the appropriate response cards and return them to the team. Ask the teams to add up the points on their cards to determine their total score. Invite the members of each team to announce how many points they received, and identify the team with the highest score as the winner.

Debriefing:

Discuss the process and the outcomes of this activity. Here are some suggested questions:

- Do you notice any interesting patterns among the application examples? What are these patterns?

- Are there similarities among applications that exemplify different values? What are these similarities?

- Which value was the most difficult one to come up with application examples for?

- Which three applications are you personally ready to implement?

Variations:

1. Stop the activity any time after the end of the second round if you are pressed for time. Immediately proceed to the evaluation round.

2. Instead of asking teams to evaluate the cards, have them prepare a consolidated list of value-application ideas from the individual cards. Each team writes its consolidated list on a flip chart and presents it to the other teams.

3. If you have fewer than six participants, play this as an individual game. Ask each participant to take a team-value envelope, write ideas on response cards, and work through the steps.

4. Change the values to ones that are more specific to your organization.

5. Repeat the activity with other activities such as customer first, openness, having fun, empowerment, and innovation.

Define the culture of your team with this interactive activity.

THE VALUES CONTINUUM
A TEAM-ASSESSMENT TOOL

Purpose:

1. To define the culture of the team
2. To develop a plan to alter the culture of the team

Team Size:

Works best with an intact team of less than 10; however, it can be adapted for use with a larger group.

Required Resources:

1. A copy of "The Values Continuum" for each person (p. 129)
2. A transparency of "The Values Continuum" (p. 129)
3. A copy of the "Culture Change Worksheet" for everyone (p. 130)
4. 3 transparencies of the "Culture Change Worksheet" (p. 130)
5. An overhead projector and screen
6. Several projector pens
7. Flip chart, pad and markers

Time:

2 hours

Room Setup:

Chairs around a U-shaped set of tables, with the overhead projector on a table at the front of the room

Steps:

1. Open the session by defining the culture of a group and outlining its importance in shaping the behavior of team members.

2. Distribute a copy of "The Values Continuum" to each team member. Display the transparency on the overhead projector. Review the directions describing how to complete the continuum.

3. Ask each person to complete the exercise. Emphasize the importance of working alone at this point.

4. If the team is small, the feedback and discussion can be done as one total group. If the group is large, use several sub-groups of five to seven members.

5. With the continuum displayed on the screen, review each item by asking where people placed their "X." Probe to uncover reasons for the placement and then facilitate a discussion of differences among team members in their perceptions of the culture.

6. As you go along, note items that seem to be in need of additional discussion because the reality of the values are different from the stated or desired culture of the team.

7. In a guided group discussion with the team, identify the top three areas that need to be addressed to help the team move closer to the desired culture. Write those areas on the flip chart.

8. Form task-teams to address the three areas by asking team members to sign up for one of the areas. Try to get a fairly even distribution across the task-teams.

9. Distribute the "Culture Change Worksheet" to each task-team and give its members 30 minutes to complete the worksheet. Provide each task-team with a transparency of the worksheet to prepare its presentation.

10. Reassemble the total team and have task-team present its report.

11. Close the session by asking each task-team to take responsibility for implementation of its recommendations. Identify a date for the team to meet again to review progress.

Variations:

1. Limit the purpose of the session to awareness of the culture. Stop at step 5 and simply summarize what has been learned at that point.

2. If time is limited, stop at step 8. Ask the task teams to compete the worksheet as a homework assignment and be prepared to report at the next meeting of the team.

3. Reduce the length of "The Values Continuum" by deleting items and keeping only those that are most relevant to your team. Applying strict relevancy criteria, you should be able to reduce the list to 10 items. This variation will also reduce the time required.

Adapted from an activity originally prepared by Sue Shanz of BOC Gases, Murray Hill, NJ.

THE VALUES CONTINUUM

Directions: Please provide your perception of the team's values by placing an "X" on each of the lines below that indicates how close the team is to one of the words/phrases on that line.

1. FORMAL ———————————————————— INFORMAL

2. STRUCTURED ———————————————— FLEXIBLE

3. INNOVATIVE ————————————————— ME-TOO

4. STRATEGIC ——————————————————— TACTICAL

5. FORGIVING ——————————————— ONE & DONE

6. SUPPORTS RISK TAKING ————————— RISK ADVERSE

7. VALUES TEAM PLAYERS ————————— VALUES LONE RANGERS

8. WELCOMES CHANGE ————————— SUPPORTS STATUS QUO

9. OUTCOME-ORIENTED —————————— ACTIVITY-BASED

10. GOES FIRST CLASS ————————————— PINCHES PENNIES

11. QUALITY IS JOB ONE ——————————— JUST GET IT DONE

12. CUSTOMERS FIRST —————————— EMPLOYEES FIRST

13. VALUES DISAGREEMENT ——————— VALUES AGREEMENT

14. WHAT YOU KNOW —————————————— WHO YOU KNOW

15. LISTENING —————————————————————— TALKING

16. HAVING FUN ——————————————— BEING SERIOUS

17. TASK-ORIENTED —————————————— PROCESS-ORIENTED

18. COLLABORATION ——————————————— COMPETITION

19. RELAXED ————————————————————— STRESSFUL

20. ETHICAL ———————————————————— QUESTIONABLE

CULTURE CHANGE WORKSHEET

1. What is the aspect of culture that is the focus of your group (e.g., conflict, quality, risk-taking)?

2. What are some examples of current team values in this area (e.g., "on this team, disagreements are aired in private or not at all")?

3. What does the team do or not do that supports these values (e.g., members who openly express dissatisfaction are frowned on by their teammates)?

4. What specific things can our team do to reduce the existing supports or encourage new positive supports (e.g., the team leader will publicly acknowledge members who express opposing points of view)?

Here's a design for a team that is under great time pressure.

TWO-HOUR TEAM BUILDING

A QUICK AND EFFECTIVE INTERVENTION

Purpose:
1. To provide a busy team with a quick intervention
2. To focus the energy of a team on specific change targets

Team Size:
Works best with an intact team of less than 10 people but can be adapted for use by a larger team

Required Resources:
1. A copy of the "Quik Team Chek" for each person (p. 133)
2. A copy of the "Two-Hour Team Building" handout for each person (p. 134)
3. A transparency of the "Quik Team Chek" with the "OK" and "NI" columns deleted
4. An overhead projector, screen, and projector pen
5. Flip chart, markers, and tape or push pins

Time:
2 1/2 hours

Room Setup:
Chairs in a circle or chairs set around a rectangular or round table

Steps:
1. Review the purpose the exercise.
2. Distribute a copy of the "Quik Team Chek" to each person.
3. Read the directions and ask if there are any questions.
4. Ask each person to complete the form.

5. Using a show of hands, tally the responses on the transparency.

6. Ask the team to select the characteristics the members want to address. Write the items selected on the flip chart leaving space between the items.

7. Ask team members to volunteer to work on one of the items selected. Write each name on the flip chart under the characteristic.

8. Distribute the "Two-Hour Team Building" handout. Ask if any items need clarification.

9. Set a date and time for the team to reconvene to hear reports from the sub-groups working on each selected characterisic.

Variations:

1. This exercise can be used in an off-site meeting. The sub-groups can go off and work for 2 hours and report back later in the day.

2. If more time exists, increase the number of items on the survey and increase the time allowed to more than 2 hours.

3. If less time is available, reduce the number of items on the survey and give the sub-groups 1 hour to come with a plan.

4. If there is only one big NI selected, keep the team together and work through the problem together.

QUIK TEAM CHEK

Directions: Please assess your team against the 10 characteristics of an effective team listed below. If you think things are satisfactory, circle OK. If you think some improvement is necessary, circle NI.

Characteristic	Circle OK or NI
1. Team goals are clear	OK NI
2. The climate is relaxed.	OK NI
3. Members are clear about their roles.	OK NI
4. Members are involved in key decisions.	OK NI
5. Team meetings are productive.	OK NI
6. Available resources are sufficient.	OK NI
7. Communication flows freely.	OK NI
8. Management supports the team.	OK NI
9. Conflicts are resolved successfully.	OK NI
10. External relationships are effective.	OK NI

TWO-HOUR TEAM BUILDING

Directions: Select one of the characteristics that needs improvement. Form a sub-group of three to five members. Devote a maximum of two hours over the next 30 days to developing an improvement plan using the format outlined below. Be prepared to report back to the team within 30 days.

1. **Problem Statement.** Prepare a crisp, one-sentence statement of the problem.

2. **Problem Analysis.** List the key causes of the problem.

3. **Alternative Solutions.** Develop a list of potential solutions to the problem.

4. **Recommendation.** Give a brief statement of your proposed solution.

5. **Implementation Plan.** List the steps involved in putting the solution into practice.

A simple but effective way to minimize role and relationship barriers.

WHAT'S MY LINE?
A ROLE-CLARIFICATION ACTIVITY

Purpose:

1. To gain clarity about team members' expectations of one another
2. To decrease the potential for role conflicts among team members
3. To increase the possibilities for collaboration among team members
4. To minimize misconceptions about team members' roles

Team Size:

Works best with an intact team of up to 8 members. If the team consists of more than 8, consider doing the activity in two segments with a break or other team activity between the segments.

Required Resources:

A copy of the "What's My Line?" handout for each team member (p. 137)

Time:

2 to 4 hours depending on the number of team members. Estimate 15 to 30 minutes per person. There will be many questions and much discussion about some roles that are not clear to everyone and little discussion about others that are clear and well known to all members.

Room Setup:

Comfortable chairs set in a circle or around a table

Steps:

1. Before the session, distribute a copy of the handout to each team member with the following instructions: "Please complete the attached form by clearly printing or typing your responses. Then make enough photocopies of the completed form for each of your teammates and bring those copies to our session on _____."

135

At the session please be prepared to present and discuss the form with your teammates. Our goal for the session is to walk away with a clear understanding of everyone's role."

2. Begin the session by reviewing the purpose and format.

3. Ask for a volunteer to be the first person to present his or her form. Alternatively, you may ask the team to decide the order of the presentations beginning with the role that will probably generate the most questions and discussion. Each person should begin by distributing a copy of his or her completed form to their teammates and then presenting the information.

4. Facilitate a discussion by asking if there are questions about any of the items or need for clarification of any of the terms. Probe for understanding and agreement from the people identified in question 3 regarding their willingness to provide the help needed.

5. Take several stretch breaks between the presentations to keep people alert and focused.

Debriefing:

Conclude the session by asking for generalizations about the value of the activity. A useful follow-up is to print and distribute a copy of the role forms to everyone.

- What was the value of the activity to you?
- How was this activity helpful to our development as a team?
- What specifically will you do differently as a result of this information?
- Who else should have access to this information (e.g., customers, senior management)?

Variations:

1. Do not distribute the completed forms as indicated in step 3. First, ask other team members how they would answer the questions on the form for this person. If there is a lack of clarity about this person's role, this variation will bring it out. Then go on to have the person distribute his or her form and present the information as indicated previously.

2. If you are not able to distribute the form in advance, run the session as an open discussion in which each person presents his or her responses to the questions and teammates ask questions. The questions can be posted on a flip chart.

WHAT'S MY LINE?

Directions: Please answer each question as specifically as possible.

1. What is your role in this team? What are the three key things you are expected to do?

2. What do you think other team members do not understand about your role?

3. What are the three most important things you need from others in the team in order to do your job in the way you would like? Be specific about what you need and, if appropriate, from whom you need it.

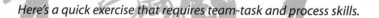

Here's a quick exercise that requires team-task and process skills.

THE WINE LIST
AN INTRODUCTORY ACTIVITY

Purpose:

1. To demonstrate the power of collaboration
2. To provide a team with a brief project that involves sharing of information, as well as planning and process skills

Team Size:

Designed for a team of 4 to 6 people. A larger group can also do this activity in series of small sub-groups.

Required Resources:

1. A deck of cards with the name of a different wine on each card (p. 140). One deck is needed for each team. Create the deck by copying page 140 on card stock and cutting it into individual cards.
2. A copy of "The Wine List" for everyone (p. 141)
3. Flip chart, pad, and markers

Time:

30 minutes

Room Setup:

Chairs set around a rectangular or round table

Steps:

1. Explain the purpose of the activity.
2. Shuffle the deck well. Place the deck face down in the middle of the table. Explain that the team's task is to organize the wines into two categories—white wines and red wines.

3. As the teams complete the activity, check their results against "The Wine List."

4. Distribute a copy of "The Wine List" to everyone.

Debriefing:

Facilitate a discussion around these questions:

- What did you do to accomplish the task?
- What was especially helpful?
- What things were not especially helpful?
- What would you do differently next time?
- How is this different or similar to the way you work "back at the ranch?"
- What did you learn about teamwork from this activity?

Post the responses to the last question on the flip chart.

Variations:

1. Turn it into a competitive game in which the first team to submit a correct list wins a prize.

2. If time permits, first have each person on the team complete the task individually. Then, ask each team to arrive at a consensus on the correct list.

3. If time permits, give each team 2 to 3 minutes to plan its approach before team members turn over the cards and begin the task.

4. If still more time is available, assign a process observer to each team to take notes on how the team worked on the task. The observers should present their feedback to each team after step 4.

Adelsheim Pinot Gris	Fessy Beaujolais	Mas de Gourgonnier Rouge
Belvedere Merlot	Forest Glen Shiraz	Peu de la Moriette Vouvray
Buena Vista Chardonnay	Jadot Bourgogne Pinot Noir	Phillips Sauvignon Blanc
Columbia Crest Cabernet Sauvignon	Jekel Johannesberg Riesling	Piccini Chianti
Dry Creek Chenin Blanc	Lamberti Pinot Grigio	Quinto de la Rosa Tinto
Duboeuf Pouilly Fuissé	Malgny Chablis	Santa Carolina Cabernet Sauvignon/Merlot

THE WINE LIST

White Wines:

- Buena Vista Chardonnay
- Malgny Chablis
- Phillips Sauvignon Blanc
- Lamberti Pinot Grigio
- Adelsheim Pinot Gris
- Dry Creek Chenin Blanc
- Peu de la Moriette Vouvray
- Duboeuf Pouilly Fuissé
- Jekel Johannesberg Riesling

Red Wines

- Forest Glen Shiraz
- Mas de Gourgonnier Rouge
- Columbia Crest Cabernet Sauvignon
- Belvedere Merlot
- Jadot Bourgogne Pinot Noir
- Piccini Chianti
- Quinto de la Rosa Tinto
- Fessy Beaujolais
- Santa Carolina Cabernet Sauvignon/Merlot

This one has multiple uses—training, assessment, planning, and even consensus-building.

WORDS TO TEAM BY
A DIFFERENT KIND OF ASSESSMENT TOOL

Purpose:

1. To help a team gain insight into some elements of its culture
2. To explore some basic team concepts such as goals, risk-taking, norms, and decision making
3. To engage in a perceptual team assessment
4. To practice consensus decision-making skills

Team Size:

Designed primarily for use with an intact team of less than 10 people; however, it can be used in an open-enrollment group to explore some basic team concepts, in which case the exercise can be done as a small group activity.

Required Resources:

1 copy of the "Words to Team By" handout for each person (p. 144)

Time:

1 hour

Room Setup:

Chairs in a circle or chairs around a rectangular or round table

Steps:

1. Clarify the purpose of the session.
2. Distribute a copy of the handout to each person. Ask the team to read the quotes and think about the meaning and/or implications of each quote for successful teamwork.

3. Facilitate a discussion of each quote beginning with this question: "What are the implications of this quote for successful teamwork?" Some other questions you might use include:

- Why is this important for a team?
- Can you give us some examples of how this works?
- What happens when this factor is not present?
- How does a team ensure that this factor is present?
- If you are the team leader, what role should you play in this area?
- If you are a team member, how can you help?

4. If you are working with an intact team, you can go on to the next phase of the exercise by asking:

- Which quote best represents our team at the present time?

5. Continuing with an intact team, you can facilitate a discussion around the following question:

- Which quote would you like to have represent us in the future? Think of it as an advertising slogan.
- Which quote would you like to see in an ad promoting our team to customers, management, and other potential team members?

6. Summarize the learning points from the exercise. In the case of an intact team, you may want to discuss "next steps" for the team in light of the results of steps and 4 and 5.

Variations:

1. In a training group, the handout can be turned into a consensus exercise. Simply ask each person to rank the quotes in terms of their importance for successful teamwork and then have each group work toward a consensus on the rankings.

2. With an intact team, the consensus activity can be "rank the quotes in terms of their importance for our success, with 1 being most important and 15 being least important." This is a double-barreled activity, because team members are discussing the concepts at the same time they are learning how to reach a consensus.

WORDS TO TEAM BY

If you don't know where you're going, any road will take you there. *Chinese proverb*	A decision is responsible when the group that makes it has to answer for it to those who are directly or indirectly affected by it. *Charles Frankel*	Never insult an alligator until you've crossed the river. *Cordell Hull*
You miss 100% of the shots you never take. *Wayne Gretzky*	A certain amount of opposition is of great help. Kites rise against, not with the wind. *John Neal*	To know the road ahead, ask those coming back. *Chinese proverb*
I don't know what the key to success is, but the key to failure is trying to please everyone. *Bill Cosby*	Don't find fault, find a remedy. *Henry Ford*	A good heart is better than all the heads in the world. *Leo Burnett*
If you obey all the rules, you miss all the fun. *Katherine Hepburn*	If you lose the power to laugh, you lose the power to think. *Clarence Darrow*	When you reach for the stars you might not get one, but you won't come up with a handful of mud either. *Leo Burnett*
Small problems are difficult to see, but easy to fix. However, when you let these problems develop, they are easy to see but difficult to fix. *Niccolo Machiavelli*	Better to ask twice than to lose your way once. *Danish proverb*	

This is a unique and fun way for team members to take a look at their team.

YOUR BLANK TEAM

AN ASSESSMENT ACTIVITY

Purpose:

To provide an intact team with an opportunity for self-assessment

Team Size:

Designed primarily for an intact team of 10 or less; however, it can also be used in a team-training class for leaders and facilitators of up to 25 participants

Required Resources:

1. A copy of "Your Blank Team" for each person (p. 147)
2. A copy of "Your Blank Team" on a transparency
3. Overhead projector, screen, and a projector pen

Time:

1 hour

Room Setup:

Chairs around a U-shaped set of tables or around a rectangular table with the overhead projector on the front table

Steps:

1. Explain the purpose of the session as a fun and different way to share our perceptions of the team.
2. Distribute the handout to each person.
3. Review the directions for completing the form. Emphasize that the exercise should be done individually at this stage.
4. If the team is small (under six), share the results as a total group. Larger groups can be divided into two sub-groups to share their perceptions.

5. Display the transparency of the handout on the projector. Ask for a volunteer (or spokesperson from one of the sub-groups) to share his or her responses. Write the words or phrases in the blanks taking one paragraph at a time. Stop when the blanks in a paragraph have been inserted, and facilitate a discussion on the extent to which other people agree with the words.

Debriefing:

Summarize the activity by asking the team to identify what it learned about the team.

- How did you feel about this exercise?
- What was its value to you as a team member?
- In what way was it helpful to the team?
- What did we learn about ourselves?
- What does the exercise tell us about our strengths?
- What does it tell us about areas we need to improve?
- What other uses does this activity have?
- How should we use the results of this exercise?

As a follow-up activity, assign individuals and/or task-teams to address the "Improvement Areas."

Variations:

1. Convert it into a fun game by using the "Your Blankety Blank Team" handout (p. 148). After that handout has been completed, display the transparency of "Your Blank Team" on the overhead and write the words in the blanks.
2. If time is limited, the handout can be completed prior to the session.

YOUR BLANK TEAM

Directions: Complete the description of your team by inserting words in the blank spaces in the paragraph below.

1. Our team is one of the _____ teams in this organization. We have _____ goals and a _____ plan to accomplish those goals.

2. The members of our team are _____ committed to working hard to accomplishing those goals by implementing the plan. Roles of team members are _____ defined. We make our decisions by the _____ method. Problems are addressed by _____ . Our operating guidelines or norms are _____ .

3. Interpersonal relationships among team members may be described as _____. Members often _____ one another. Members _____ active listening to ensure accurate communication. Conflict is resolved by _____.

4. Team meetings always start _____. There is _____ an agenda for the meeting. Meetings are opportunities for members to _____ . Members usually feel the meetings are a _____ experience.

5. Management's support for the team is characterized by _____ . When the team needs resources to get the job done, it can count on management to _____ . The team is empowered by management to _____ .

6. The future of the team is _____ . At this point the team should _____ . I am personally very _____ with my participation on the team and look forward to _____ in the future.

YOUR BLANKETY BLANK TEAM

Directions: Do not look at the other handout before completing this activity. Provide the words requested. Humor is encouraged.

Paragraph 1

1. Adjective _____
2. Large Number _____
3. Adjective _____

Paragraph 2

4. Adverb _____
5. Adverb _____
6. Name of an animal _____
7. Noun _____
8. Adjective _____

Paragraph 3

9. Adjective _____
10. Verb _____
11. Verb _____
12. Form of punishment _____

Paragraph 4

13. Adverb _____
14. Adverb _____
15. Verb_____
16. Adjective _____

Paragraph 5

17. Type of Mental Illness _____
18. Verb _____
19. Verb _____

Paragraph 6

20. Weather report (one or two words) _____
21. Verb _____
22. Verb (ending in "ied") _____
23. Name of animal (plural) _____

Here's a team assessment that doesn't use a written survey form.

YOUR TAROT TEAM
A QUICK TEAM ASSESSMENT

Purpose:

1. To conduct a quick assessment of the team by members of the team
2. To give members an opportunity to describe their goals for their teams

Team Size:

Designed for an intact team of less than 10. The exercise can also be used in a training session for team leaders.

Required Resources:

A deck of Tarot cards for each team. Tarot cards are available in game stores, new age book stores, and other similar outlets. The *Albano-Waite Tarot* is published by U. S. Games Systems, Inc., 179 Ludlow Street, Stamford, CT 06902, 1-203-353-8400.

Time:

30 to 45 minutes depending on the size of the team

Room Setup:

Chairs in a circle or chairs around a rectangular or round table

Steps:

1. Explain the purpose of the activity as a quick and fun way to take a look at our team now and in the future.
2. Shuffle the cards well. Distribute five to seven cards to each team member. Place the remaining cards in the middle of the table. Ask each person to privately select one card that represents his or her perception of the team now and then one card that represents his or her hopes for the team in the future. If desired, he or she may discard one of the cards (placing it at the bottom of the deck in the middle of the table) and take another from the top of the deck.

3. Begin with perceptions of the team today. Ask each team member to show his or her card and explain (1) why he/she picked the card and (2) how it represents the team today. Probe for reasons behind the selections.

4. Move on to the hopes for the future. Ask each person to show that card and again explain his or her reasons for the selection. And once again, probe for reasons for the selection.

5. Facilitate a discussion of the outcomes of the exercise and possible next steps. For example, the team may want to conduct a more formal written assessment or go on to planning that focuses on current issues and actions required to reach the future goals.

Variations:

1. Change the focus of the exercise to individual assessment. Each person selects a card that represents how he/she sees him-/herself now and one card that represents how he or she would like to be seen.

2. Change the focus to individual feedback. Divide into dyads or triads and give each sub-group a bunch of cards. Place the cards face up on the table. Members pick the card or cards that they believe represents the other person(s) in the sub-group and explain why they picked it. They are encouraged to be as specific as possible. If the team is small enough, the exercise can be done as one group.

Address destructive internal competition with this game.

ZERO SUM?
A CROSS-TEAM COLLABORATION GAME

Purpose:
To discourage teams from automatically competing with one another

Team Size:
Works best with 3 to 5 teams, each with 2 to 7 members

Required Resources:
1. "Triplets Puzzle Sheet" (see "Preparations" section below) (pp. 154–155)
2. "Team Instructions Sheet" (p. 153)
3. Timer
4. Whistle

Time:
20 minutes

Room Setup:
Chairs around a rectangular or round table for each team

Preparation:
1. Review the "Triplets Puzzle Sheet" and solve the puzzle. Check with the correct answers on page 156.
2. Prepare a puzzle sheet for each team. Write the first two letters of the link word in the blanks for a few triplets in each sheet in such a way that no two puzzle sheets contain the same clues and that when all the sheets are combined, clues for every triplet are provided.

Steps:

1. Explain how to solve a triplet puzzle. Use the examples given on page 154. Write the triplets on a flip chart and demonstrate how the first one is done. Coach the participants to solve the second one. Present the third one and let them solve it by themselves.

2. Distribute the "Triplets Puzzle Sheet" and the "Team Instructions Sheet" to each team. Set the timer and blow the whistle. Announce that you are timing the activity.

3. The main point of the activity is that teams assume that they are competing with one another (even though the instructions do not say so). If anyone asks for clarification of the rules, refer him or her back to the "Team Instructions Sheet." In the unlikely event that the teams collaborate with one another, neither discourage nor encourage them.

4. Blow the whistle at the end of 5 minutes. Announce the conclusion of the game. Ask if any team has solved the puzzle. Congratulate this team. If no team has solved the puzzle, identify and congratulate the team with the most triplets solved.

Debriefing:

Ask the participants what prevented the teams from collaborating with one another. Discuss the responses and follow up with these questions:

- In a zero-sum game, only one team can win. What makes us conclude that all team activities are zero-sum games?

- How would your behavior have changed if the instructions clearly stated that more than one team could win and recommended a collaborative technique?

- If your corporation has different teams serving the same (or similar) function, would they automatically compete with one another?

- What teams do you currently belong to? Do they compete with other teams? Can your team gain something by cooperating with other teams?

- What are some techniques for successfully collaborating with other teams?

Varations:

Use a crossword puzzle or a cryptogram instead of the triplets puzzle. Make sure that each team is provided with different sets of clues.

- Appoint a few participants as observers. Ask them to record team behaviors using the "Observer's Guidelines" (p. 157).

TEAM INSTRUCTIONS SHEET

Directions:
- All teams have the *same* puzzle sheet but each team has a *different* set of clues.
- Find the link word for each triplet and write it in the appropriate blank.
- After you have solved all the triplets, copy the first letters of the link words. You will get an important message about teams.

Time Limit:

You have 5 minutes to solve the puzzle.

Scoring:
- If your team solves the puzzle in 3 minutes, you get 10 points.
- If your team solves the puzzle in 5 minutes, you get 5 points.

TRIPLETS PUZZLE SHEET

A *triplet* is a set of three words that are linked by a common fourth word. For example:

ELEPHANT - HOUSE - SNOW

What word links these three words? The linking word should appear before or after each of the three words to form well-known compound words or phrases.

    The correct answer for this triplet is WHITE, as in WHITE ELEPHANT, WHITE HOUSE, and SNOW WHITE.

    Here are three more triplets. See if you can find the linking word for each of them. Remember that the linking word may appear either before or after each word in the triplet.

BOARD - HOLE - JACK
DOUBLE - ROAD - STITCH
MAKER - TENNIS - STICK

Here are the correct solutions:

BLACK (BLACKBOARD, BLACK HOLE, BLACKJACK)
CROSS (DOUBLE CROSS, CROSSROAD, and CROSSTITCH)
MATCH (MATCH MAKER, TENNIS MATCH, MATCH STICK)

See the next page for more triplets. Determine the linking word for each triplet, and write it in the appropriate blank. After you have solved all the triplets, read the first letters of the link words for an important message.

TRIPLETS PUZZLE SHEET

_____ 1. REIN - HUNTER - SKIN

_____ 2. RIG - CRUDE - SNAKE

_____ 3. BAD - BULLETIN - FLASH

_____ 4. ROBBERY - EXPRESS - WAGON

_____ 5. CHEESE - ICE - SOUR

_____ 6. SECOND - POLL - PUBLIC

_____ 7. BELT - BLOOD - ORDER

_____ 8. BRUSH - OIL - SPRAY

_____ 9. DOUBLE - LEVEL - BLANK

_____ 10. AGREEMENT - FREE - SECRET

_____ 11. FIRE - ARTIST - NARROW

_____ 12. DUTY - RADIO - VOICE

_____ 13. WEAR - WATER - TAKER

_____ 14. GROUP - GUIDE - PACKAGE

_____ 15. COUPLE - JOB - NUMBER

_____ 16. MAN - BITTER - CABINET

_____ 17. INSURANCE - ORANGE - SECRET

_____ 18. LIFE - LIMIT - PART

_____ 19. AGE - PUMPING - WAFFLE

_____ 20. INSTANT - READY - VIDEO

_____ 21. FARM - CRACKERS - PARTY

_____ 22. READING - STICK - UPPER

_____ 23. PAINS - UNION - MANUAL

_____ 24. SUBMARINE - FEVER - JACKET

TRIPLETS PUZZLE ANSWERS

DEER_____ 1. REIN - HUNTER - SKIN

OIL_____ 2. RIG - CRUDE - SNAKE

NEWS_____ 3. BAD - BULLETIN - FLASH

TRAIN_____ 4. ROBBERY - EXPRESS - WAGON

CREAM_____ 5. CHEESE - ICE - SOUR

OPINION_____ 6. SECOND - POLL - PUBLIC

MONEY_____ 7. BELT - BLOOD - ORDER

PAINT_____ 8. BRUSH - OIL - SPRAY

ENTRY_____ 9. DOUBLE - LEVEL - BLANK

TRADE_____ 10. AGREEMENT - FREE - SECRET

ESCAPE_____ 11. FIRE - ARTIST - NARROW

ACTIVE_____ 12. DUTY - RADIO - VOICE

UNDER_____ 13. WEAR - WATER - TAKER

TOUR_____ 14. GROUP - GUIDE - PACKAGE

ODD_____ 15. COUPLE - JOB - NUMBER

MEDICINE_____ 16. MAN - BITTER - CABINET

AGENT_____ 17. INSURANCE - ORANGE - SECRET

TIME_____ 18. LIFE - LIMIT - PART

IRON_____ 19. AGE - PUMPING - WAFFLE

CAMERA_____ 20. INSTANT - READY - VIDEO

ANIMAL_____ 21. FARM - CRACKERS - PARTY

LIP_____ 22. READING - STICK - UPPER

LABOR_____ 23. PAINS - UNION - MANUAL

YELLOW_____ 24. SUBMARINE - FEVER - JACKET

OBSERVER'S GUIDELINES

Directions: Please sit where you can see and hear most of the team discussions. You are a silent observer—do not speak or in any way participate in the activity. Take notes. Use quotes that demonstrate a point.

1. **Task Behaviors.** What things helped or hindered the team in its effort to get the job done?

2. **Process Behaviors.** What things helped or hindered the way the team worked together?

3. **Competitive Behaviors.** What types of things did the team do to compete with the other teams?

4. **Collaborative Behaviors.** What types of things did the team do to collaborate with the other teams?

Topical Index of Games and Activities

Activities and Games: Primary Use

Activity	Team Building	Team Training
BALLOONATICS	X	
BOXED IN	X	X
BUILDING BRIDGES	X	
CENSORSHIP	X	
CONTROVERSY	X	X
DEFINING MOMENT	X	
ESCAPE FROM GILLIGAN'S ISLAND	X	X
ET		X
FREE CASH	X	X
HELP!		X
HOW DO YOU LIKE YOUR RECOGNITION?	X	X
METCALFE		X
OUR TEAM		X
QUOTES FROM EXPERTS		X
REAL VIRTUAL		X
SDLT	X	X
SITUATION ANALYSIS		X
SLEEPLESS IN SEATTLE		X
SLOGANS	X	X
STAGES		X
TEAM BINGO		X
TEAM CONTEST	X	
TEAM DECISIONS		X
TEAM GAME SHOW		X
TEAM HATS	X	
TEAM LEADER		X
TEAM NORMS		X
TEAM QUOTES		X
TEAM REWARDS	X	X
TEAM VALUES		X
THE VALUES CONTINUUM	X	
TWO-HOUR TEAM BUILDING	X	
WHAT'S MY LINE?	X	
WINE LIST		X
WORDS TO TEAM BY	X	
YOUR BLANK TEAM	X	
YOUR TAROT TEAM	X	
ZERO SUM?		X

Activities and Games: Time and Participants

Activity	Time	Number of Participants
BALLOONATICS	30–45 minutes	Any number
BOXED IN	30 minutes	4–6
BUILDING BRIDGES	2–2.5 hours	10 or fewer
CENSORSHIP	15 minutes–1 hour	4–7
CONTROVERSY	45 minutes	Six or more
DEFINING MOMENT	1 hour	10 or fewer
ESCAPE FROM GILLIGAN'S ISLAND	1.5–2 hours	10 or fewer
ET	45 minutes	10-50
FREE CASH	30–45 minutes	9
HELP!	15–20 minutes	4–6
HOW DO YOU LIKE YOUR RECOGNITION?	1 hour	10 or fewer
METCALFE	30 minutes	10 or more
OUR TEAM	45 minutes	12–30
QUOTES FROM EXPERTS	30–45 minutes	3–7
REAL VIRTUAL	60–90 minutes	9 or more
SDLT	45 minutes	12–20
SITUATION ANALYSIS	45 minutes–1 hour	4–6
SLEEPLESS IN SEATTLE	60–90 minutes	12–30
SLOGANS	30–45 minutes	Fewer than 10
STAGES	45 minutes	More than 9
TEAM BINGO	30 minutes	Any
TEAM CONTEST	90 minutes	10–30
TEAM DECISIONS	45 minutes	9–30
TEAM GAME SHOW	30–45 minutes	25–35
TEAM HATS	30 minutes	More than 10
TEAM LEADER	45 minutes	15–30
TEAM NORMS	30–45 minutes	10 or more
TEAM QUOTES	30–45 minutes	More than 15
TEAM REWARDS	2 hours	10 or fewer
TEAM VALUES	45 minutes	8–30
THE VALUES CONTINUUM	2 hours	Fewer than 10
TWO-HOUR TEAM BUILDING	2.5 hours	Fewer than 10
WHAT'S MY LINE?	2–4 hours	10 or fewer
WINE LIST	30 minutes	4–6
WORDS TO TEAM BY	1 hour	Fewer than 10
YOUR BLANK TEAM	1 hour	Fewer than 10
YOUR TAROT TEAM	30–45 minutes	Fewer than 10
ZERO SUM?	20 minutes	6–35